"*Resilience: Living Life by Design* demonstrates how female leaders can boost their self-esteem, bolster their self-confidence, and defy adversity against all odds."

- **Barbara Corcoran**, Real Estate Mogul, Business Expert and Shark on ABC's *Shark Tank*

"*Resilience* is a powerful journey of self-discovery that teaches us how the strength of steel comes from being in the fire. Dr. Deana illustrates how some of life's most profound, core-shaking lessons come disguised as tragedies, all meant to show us how strong we really are. Through *Resilience* we learn to embrace every day as the once in a lifetime opportunity to be authentically, triumphantly alive."

- **Blondell Reynolds Brown**, Philadelphia City Councilwoman at-Large

"Dr. Deana Murphy has done it again! Her talent and gifting for helping women live a "remarkable" life has brought together an inspiring group of voices and stories. Her newest book, *Resilience* does a wonderful job of using everyday stories to help everyday women live extraordinary lives. God intends that we live life by divine design. This book shows you how. Don't just read it—devour it—and make sure you share it!"

- **Marshawn Evans Daniels**, Reinvention Strategist & Godfidence Coach, TV Personality from *The Apprentice* & Miss America Finalist; Godfidence.com

"What makes one woman give in to failure and another rise up and succeed against the odds? The stories of the 12 women in *Resilience: Living Life by Design* teach how to use purpose, courage, and faith to find your way as a leader, entrepreneur, and life traveler. The book shows you how all of your experiences are designed to help you create a full and successful life, no matter how dark they may seem in the moment. The stories are as useful as they are inspiring. I will keep it close to me to grab whenever I need to ignite my heart."

- **Marcia Reynolds, PsyD**, author of *Wander Woman*, and *The Discomfort Zone: How Leaders Turn Difficult Conversations into Breakthroughs*; former president of the International Coach Federation

"We must tell our stories, since we learn from our past and carve the trail for future generations. Like a beacon of light, Dr. Deana Murphy serves as a guidepost for empowerment and coupled with 12 women's messages of hopeful inspiration. A must read for thought leaders and entrepreneurs."

- **Laura Ponticello**, Visionary and Publisher, Divine Phoenix Books, and author of *Live the Life of Your Dreams*: *33 Tips for Inspired Living*

"Nothing inspires us more than people who learn how to tap into their inner strength to overcome obstacles and to live their life on purpose. *Resilience* is a must-read if your heart wonders if you can safely cross the bridge to get to the other side of possibility. *Resilience* will inspire you and help you to discover that 'There Is More Inside'--You!"

- **S. Renee Smith**, Nationally Recognized Self-Esteem and Branding Expert & Coach, Speaker & Author

"Dr. Deana Murphy's *Resilience: Living Life By Design* is an amazing testimony to the power of being resilient. Discover your true value and purpose in life and how faith, perseverance and patience can carry you through your toughest life experiences. Through the powerful stories presented, you will learn how to gain renewed vision, and find a new sense of freedom to live life as God has intended despite the challenges you face."

- **Monica Davis**, president of Atela Productions, Inc., Publisher of *Exceptional People Magazine*, and best-selling business author of *Welcome to the Top* and *Start Your Business Right*.

"*Resilience: Living Life By Design* is a journey through the lives of 12 remarkable women that encourages, uplifts, and engages. If you hope to flourish despite tough circumstances, this book will encourage you with compelling narratives and practical tips to guide your next steps."

- **Glenda Wrenn, MD, MSHP.**, Assistant Professor of Clinical Psychiatry, Director, Division of Behavioral Health Satcher Health Leadership Institute Morehouse School of Medicine

Published by : Publishing for Women by Women
a division of Dr. Deana Unlimited, LLC.
P.O. Box 414, Horsham, PA 19044-3408
www.DeanaMurphyGlobal.com
www.TheResilienceBook.com

Printed in the United States of America

ISBN-13: 978—0-9864015-0-3
ISBN-10: 0986401501
1. Personal Transformation 2. Women in Business 3. Self-Help Motivation 4. Well-being

Scripture quotations labeled MSG are taken from *The Message* by Eugene H. Patterson, copyright ©1993, 1994, 1995 2000, 2001, 2002. Use by permission of NavPress Publishing Group. All rights reserved.

Edited in parts by Eagle Eye Editing and Proofreading Services.

The information, tips and strategies offered in this book are the result of the practical application and experiences of the author and its contributors and are intended only for pursuing and building resilience—seeking and developing a positive outlook, acquiring a sense of personal mastery, fostering active engagement and finding meaning in the events of adversity, setbacks and/or distress, and are not a repacement for professional medical advice or therapy. Publishing by Women for Women and the author makes no representations or warranties that any individual will achieve a particular result.

RESILIENCE

LIVING LIFE BY DESIGN

DR. DEANA MURPHY

WITH EXPERIENCES OF

12 Remarkable Women

Publishing By Women for Women

Horsham, Pennsylvania

These LifeDesigns come together to tell an aesthetically appealing story of faith.

This book is dedicated to:

The Ultimate Designer of all life—thank you for honoring me with the vision and task of compiling a blueprint from which others can design their lives where positive change and maximizing potential can be their norm. I am humbled by this assignment and will endeavor to bring only you glory through it.

To women leaders everywhere—life is too short to be something you are not. *Be the leader. Do not settle. Create positive change.*

Contents

Prologue

Having survived a near fatal car accident at age 20, I encountered an unexpected lesson in adaptation to life. Although, my journey was experienced through the lens of a deep, personal faith, I have often reflected on how exactly I was able to respond to such adversity with a positive outcome. As I went on to pursue medical school, and eventual training in psychiatry and health policy research, my main focus was building a good life and restoring my hopes and dreams despite my limitations and disAbility.

I was grateful for the talent, optimism, confidence, faith, family, and friends that sustained me throughout multiple surgeries and months of physical therapy. But with later encounters as a physician with community members, consumers of health care services, and high-performing colleagues, who were broken and suffering (often in silence), I returned to unanswered questions about how best to promote positive outcomes to stress for others.

We enter this world endowed with the capacity to love and thrive. It is our natural inheritance of resilience, existing at a cellular as well as metaphysical level. Often, we are unaware of and take for granted the capacity to adapt and overcome. When adversity comes into uncertain, unpredictable environments, our biobehavioral systems are particularly stressed and strained—challenging that capacity. Post-traumatic stress disorder and depression are two outcomes of facing adversity, however the most common response to extreme stressors is in fact, recovery and resilience. Some individuals even experience post-traumatic growth. What can we learn from the stories of everyday and uncommon resilience in the face of adversity?

The scientific study of resilience began with an attempt to understand children who emerged from environments of severe stress relatively intact. Positive social relationships and effective actions in the environment, such as school achievement, were identified protective factors for children. Although we are learning more each day, less is known about what contributes to the development of resilience in adults. In addition, much focus and attention remains on symptoms and disorders that reflect a failure of adaptation to life's demands, but there is much to be gained from careful reflection and inquiry into the skills that enable successful resilience in the face of life's challenges.

Our ongoing research seeks to intervene to promote resilience, building on the science that has revealed that exceptional survival is linked to *goal-directed action* whereas traumatic stress is typified by the more reactive *stimulus-based responding* (Kent, Rivers, Wrenn 2015).[1] To use an analogy, becoming a thermostat is more resilient than remaining a thermometer. Our capacity to change and continually grow using the nutrients of faith, inspiration, replacing unhelpful thinking, and correcting deficits in neurotransmitters using medications or neuromodulation are all important pathways to recovery and resilience.

Resilience: Living Life By Design is a journey through the lives of 12 remarkable women that encourages, uplifts, and engages. What these women have discovered through wisdom of lived-experience will help you think about your own definitions of resilience. We all have a story of resilience waiting to be told. You may be in the arc of adversity, at the peak of persecution. If so, I hope you will find encouragement and strength in applying the tips and truths presented here to your current circumstance.

For those of us who live in environments of peak performance and elite execution, it is important to recognize that cultivating resilience often requires asking for help, admitting vulnerability, and accepting our own failure. Invincibility is not required for resilience, and strong survivors are not always thriving.

If you hope to flourish despite tough circumstances, this book will encourage you with compelling narratives and practical tips to guide your next steps. The reality of resilience as accessible and achievable is a message of hope that is also grounded in compelling science. But since stories are much more emotionally powerful than research papers, I am really glad you have decided to take this journey to discovering your path to living a resilient life by design.

Glenda Wrenn, MD., MSHP., Assistant Professor of Clinical Psychiatry, Director, Division of Behavioral Health Satcher Health Leadership Institute Morehouse School of Medicine

Works Cited

[1]**Kent, Martha; Rivers, Crystal T.; Wrenn, Glenda. 2015.** "Goal-Directed Resilience in Training (GRIT) Behav. Sci. 5, no. 2: 264-304.

Acknowledgements

My motivation and dedication for living life by design and the appreciation and support of the concept came from multiple sources that have significantly touched my heart:

All of my creativity, inspiration and zeal begins and ends with God—the author and finisher of my faith.

The 12 remarkable women who contributed to this book—Angela M. Brown, Angeline Lawrence, Denise Hanney, Diane Blake, Fayola Delica, Glenda O. Cook, Gwen Webber-McLeod, Kim Cheatham, Mabel Jones-Hansford, Mellanie Kai Lassiter, Teresita Glasgow and Valeria Robinson-Baker—whose determination and drive turned their plight into a power move.

Danielle Elyse helped me view many occurrences through the lens of a different perspective. Expertise, efficiency and excellence describe her high-standard approach to her work.

Dr. Lucile Richardson, whose consultancy, encouragement and support guided and kept me compliant through this project.

Alexia Renee'—nothing short of exceptional design and layout skills. Patience and attention to detail are your strengths.

My committed, trusting and sometimes shattered clients I had the wonderful honor to come along side of over the years. I saw the deliberate determination to live what they thought was impossible.

The one who makes my heart sing and feet dance—my husband Eric. I could not have done this and many of the things I do without you.

My special children—Tishay, Isaiah and Joshua—I love you more.

Introduction

MESSAGE FROM THE PUBLISHER

Like you, I have experienced many setbacks.

What is the one word that describes you?" When this question was presented to an audience of over 500 women, and a few men, I heard a voice behind me shout, "Resilient!" I thought, of course, that's me! My mind began to churn. I instantly recalled different incidents that had turned my world upside down. In the same moment I came back to what it was that prepared me to get up from my valley. And then it hit me. My inner strength—a wellspring of resilience and relentless desire to be the leader who was determined to not settle.

I could not seem to shake that encounter. Shortly afterward, the idea for this book was conceived. I thought about other women who may have suffered hopelessness and helplessness; those inescapable daily difficulties—the loss of a job, the client who quits, the wayward child, the spouse walking out, the negative medical report or the death of a loved one. In the end, we want to make it all go away. We want to be strong. Whole. Complete. We truly want to be resilient, but how?

It is said resilience is the ability to bounce back when faced with difficult or painful situations. But do we really bounce back from these hardships? I would say not. Inevitably we must move through them—from sorrow to satisfaction, from pain to purpose, from trials to triumphs, from suffering to success—discovering on the other side of adversity the hard-won wisdom and meaning of it all. In the fact sheet for psychologists working with adults, resilience is defined as an interactive product of beliefs, attitudes, approaches, behaviors and perhaps physiology that help people fare better during adversity and recover more quickly following it.[1] We must trust our own abilities and use our strengths to live successful, positive lives.

When I discovered I was being downsized from my executive position at a Fortune 500 institution, with both a bitter and sweet defiance, I knew I had come to the end of my corporate career. When life presents a loss, it is easy to lose ourselves. If not careful, we can become prone to a vexation to the soul and eaten by fear. As a lone woman in the department, I often experienced a false feeling of inadequacy. Still I learned to put my tenacity to work in order to survive what I later discovered was only an illusion. A senseless emotion.

> When life presents a loss, it is easy to lose ourselves.

The intelligent, resourceful and courageous side of me longed to ask myself some tough questions. What was my heart saying?

With a longing to increase the value in others, I always desired to succeed as an entrepreneur. Leaving my corporate position undoubtedly presented the opportunity. I learned to be flexible in attaining this goal but had not factored in the many obstacles that were lurking—bankruptcy, homelessness, falsely accused in an unlawful conspiracy and even being robbed at knifepoint. No doubt this unforeseen consequence was a hurtful and embarrassing season, but not once (that I can recall) did I succumb to self-pity or question God.

Part of my life's work was teaching women how to design their lives—push past their fears, build resilience, unleash their best within and enjoy more life. It was paradoxical to be faced with the challenge of redesigning the fragments of my own life by the very lessons I taught. The challenge was keeping my mind intact and not engaging in a self-defeating dialogue with my inner critic. Remembering how I taught others to not be influenced by their belittling inner speech, I was determined to not fall prey to it either. But was I a leader of influence? Through soul-searching and meditation I discovered my uninspiring truth—I was unsure and insecure. I was stuck. Perhaps this describes you.

Sustained by my faith, I remember crying out to God, "What are you telling me to do? Make it plain to me so I can understand!" While in my kitchen one morning desperately seeking Him for direction, I clearly heard a whisper in my spirit, "Elevate, educate and motivate my people." Often this passage comes to mind and to this day it keeps me strong:

> "And I am convinced and sure of this very thing, that He Who began a good work in you will continue until the day of Jesus Christ right up to the time of His return, developing that good work and perfecting and bringing it to full completion in you." Philippians 1:6, (*AMP)*.

Through struggle I learned how to embrace positive change.

In moving through these conditions, I became a serial entrepreneur attaining international recognition; quoted in newspapers, books and magazines including *O* Magazine; serving on boards; receiving awards and making national television appearances. In disabling and dismantling the horrendous conditions I faced, I built a new resilience.

We all have an interest in resilience because we have encountered demanding life events. In spite of them we have by God's grace managed to persevere and sustain. My own events, my interest in the topic of resilience, together with these collective personal experiences and especially the woman leader who, like me, masks her pain in her corner office or the boardroom, gave me the impetus for moving forward to direct and publish this anthology.

The Intention of this Book

No matter where you are today, you have untapped potential that will take you everywhere you want to go. The goal of this book is helping you get there. From the experiences of 12 women, this compilation speaks to talented women leaders and entrepreneurs with the purpose of helping to turn their restlessness into a strategy and showing them how to maintain their spiritual and emotional center during hardship.

> No matter where you are today, you have untapped potential that will take you everywhere you want to go.

Their stories are not based on research, lab work or theory. These 12 women, like me, derived heartfelt meaning from painful situations. They share a common history of some sort of trauma. Their chronicles are birthed from a desire to galvanize themselves in effectively and successfully tackling problems. They share experiences, not as passive victims of their past, but proactive designers of their future. The book is centered on turning a plight into a power move. This collaboration is purposed to give voice to suffered anxieties so other women leaders may learn from their well-thought-out actions, rise above negative perspectives, thrive under pressure and maximize career and personal performances.

Everyone needs resilience, an essential component of leadership. All women are resilient, but some need others to show them how this virtue is developed. A human quality rooted in a person's existence, resilience remodels, renews and restores the soul. It remodels the hardship into the challenge. It renews the victim into the survivor. It restores power to the helpless. Regardless of your social status, financial position or relational connections, your true ally is resilience.

So how can you be more resilient? Firstly, your strength acts as an inner engine that determines how far you go in the midst of life's hurdles. Secondly, your personal empowerment contends you always have choices and are capable to see life's most challenging circumstances as opportunities for growth and expanding your wisdom. Resilience is undoubtedly the backbone of success.

Resilience is undoubtedly the backbone of success.

The more I observe human nature, the more convinced I am that most women are unprepared to manage the effects of adversity. Considering the impact a setback has on your thoughts, actions, emotional and physical health, the accounts of the women here will guide you in cultivating and training your inner strength and putting it to work for you.

You may not be able to change the situation, but you can work on the notion of changing yourself. You are born empowered to build resilience.

Resilience: Living Life by Design is a collaborative call to female leaders who perceive who they are, understand the needs that drive their decisions, discover new ways to direct their lives, design lives of purpose, and intentionally plan their futures—whether scaling the corporate ladder, venturing out as an entrepreneur, ministering in the community or running their households.

What You Will Find in This Book

Many female leaders hide behind a façade of their past, profiling the false image that all is well while secretly pursuing answers and direction outside of themselves. Each story you read describes how focusing on the greater good within is needed in designing the life you have always desired, no matter what.

You will discover how to face problematic issues head-on with a confident attitude that in the end, self-love and forgiveness conquer. This book also advocates self-evaluation—measuring yourself through the characteristics of your faith instead of through the character of others. Every chapter highlights personal transformation—shifting your mindset to the possibilities beyond your perspective. These triumphant stories embody practicing thriving instead of surviving, leveraging each experience for personal growth and achievement.

You may even find yourself among the pages.

It seems that resilience has as many definitions as people who define it, not to mention the fact that resilience has personal meanings as well. In this collection of narratives, each contributor shares her own **distinguished definition of resilience** originated from her experiences.

After reading *Resilience*, you will know how to:

- **Recognize and remove the enemies of resilience**—the unhelpful thoughts, actions and reactions, or the outside obstacles that automatically show up to influence you.

- Override destructive behavior by **turning reactions into resilience**—learning to live with intention by letting go of what you cannot control and living in harmony with what you can.

- Build resilience through **the power of living life by design** so you can realize a sense of purpose and reach higher levels of identity and self-actualization, letting go of victim-consciousness and accepting personal responsibility.

- **Pursue resilience** by developing the attributes of self-awareness, patience, perseverance, inner power and becoming action-oriented to successfully advance after adversity.

While reading through these pages seeking direction for the edginess in your personal and professional journeys, here are some questions I want you to personally consider:

1. What is the hidden opportunity and where can it lead?
2. What has the setback shown you that needs changing?
3. What are the best lessons learned? How will you implement these lessons for change?
4. What will be your new normal?

I have also appended a simple resilience exercise to the back of this book for helping you with answers to the above questions intended to elevate, educate and motivate you.

God wants to develop and perfect the good work in you and bring it to full completion. Your picking up this book is an indication there is more in you to grow and give. You can move past insecurities, uncertainties and get unstuck so you can give to others the amazing life designed for you.

I hope the women you meet here will mentor you each time you read their stories. My earnest desire is by adopting their practical lifestyle strategies, you will experience every benefit that comes from living with determination, spirituality, love and resilience.

Be the leader. Never settle. Create positive change.

I am honored and happy to present *Resilience: Living Life by Design.*

Dr. Deana Murphy, Dr. Deana Unlimited, LLC. and
Publishing by Women for Women,
www.CallDrDeana.com

Works Cited

[1]**Lisa D. Butler, PhD, Stanford University; Stevan E. Hobfoll, PhD, Kent State University; Terence M. Keane, PhD, VA Boston Healthcare System:** Fostering Resilience in Response to Terrorism: A Fact Sheet for Psychologist Working With Adults. http://www.deep.med.miami.edu/media/FostResilRspTerAdltsAPA.pdf

ONE

Turning Obstacles Into Opportunities
BY ANGELA M. BROWN

Defining Resilience

Proverbs 24:10 (*ESV*) reads, "If you faint in the day of adversity, your strength is small." Another version of this same proverb is less gracious and simply states, "If you fall to pieces in a crisis, there wasn't much to you in the first place" (*MSG*).

While most of us are proud to tout our accomplishments as a testament to who we are, the truest measurement of what we are made of is not what we do, but how we respond to the challenges that bring us face to face with our fears. This, for me, epitomizes resilience—the ability to bounce back from adversity, allowing the obstacles in our lives to reveal who we really are, instead of conforming us into who we are not.

My Story

I have certainly journeyed the road less traveled. It was not a freshly paved road either, but one shaped by adversity. For me that journey began in 1989 when, at the age of 17, I arrived at a fork in the road while on scholarship at the prestigious Hampton University. There, as a college freshman, I discovered I was pregnant. Having vowed after my parents' divorce I would never wed or have children, I found myself at a defining moment in my life—one I realized would not only shape my destiny, but that of my unborn child.

Deciding to be the wife and mother God saw me being instead of the one I feared I would become, I elected to take a detour after my first semester, deciding to marry and give birth to my first child.

If I were to rip a page from my journal at the time, it would probably read like Charles Dickens' *A Tale of Two Cities*:

> It was the best of times, it was the worst of times, it was the age of wisdom, it was the age of foolishness, it was the epoch of belief, it was the epoch of incredulity, it was the season of Light, it was the season of Darkness, it was the spring of hope, it was the winter of despair, we had everything before us, we had nothing before us.[1]

I have since learned that it simply was *my* time.

Do not misunderstand—it was *the* scariest time of my life! Having to face my father and tell him his baby girl was dropping out of college to get married because she was pregnant caused me many a sleepless night. Not only was I facing the biggest obstacle of my newly minted adult life, most would surmise *I* was the obstacle!

Nonetheless, I faced my father and the circumstances confronting me, and the scariest time of my life became a pivotal moment as I learned to turn obstacles into opportunities by facing adversity, not running from it. I have since gone on to obtain my degree, start and run a successful public relations firm, host a talk show and rake in awards, appointments and speaking engagements in recognition of my professional success. Yet my proudest achievements and source of the happiest, most fulfilling moments of my life remain my marriage of 25 years and the two beautiful children it gave birth to—the very things I feared and avoided the most.

Recognizing and Removing the Enemies of Resilience

Too often we avoid the people, places and experiences we fear and, in doing so, forfeit discovery of who we really are, the life we were designed to live and the impact we were created to have—all because we will not give up the reins. This is true of even the highest-achieving women, those of us who spend so much time "doing" that we neglect "being." The fact is, we are usually the least willing to surrender control and most guilty of statements beginning with "I will never ..." as in "I will never allow anyone to do that to me" or "I will never go back there." However, I have learned the "I will never" areas in our lives are where our fears reside, and those who fear vulnerability and risk never reach their full potential.

> I have learned the "I will never" areas in our lives are where our fears reside...

Throughout the early years of my marriage, we struggled financially—a lot. Often, it merely resulted from the fact that we lived off one income as I balanced going back to college and rearing children while my husband worked to provide for our family. Yet whenever there was a shortfall—and there were many—my fears surfaced, masked as "I will never depend upon a man," and pushed me flailing into self-survival mode, blaming my husband and preparing to take flight.

Had I left, I would have forfeited some of the most rewarding experiences of my life, and more importantly, the most meaningful relationships in my life. That is exactly what fear exists to do, rob us of the future we want by holding us hostage to the past we do not.

Women are the "ribs;" we not only hold up, we hold it down!

Could I have left, found a job and taken care of my children and myself? Of course I could—I am a woman. Women are the "ribs;" we not only hold up, we hold it down! We are also flexible, adaptable and designed to cover and protect what is most vulnerable and vital. Resilient women understand this, refusing to allow hurts of the past to cause them to become bitter and rigid. The rigid break. The resilient know how to hold on *and* when to let go—a lesson I learned from my husband.

Turning Reactions into Resilience

Early in my career, I was recruited by a top-ten public relations firm, attracted not only by the money and prestige a position there offered, but the promise of a shorter commute as I sought to bring more balance to my family and professional life.

Shortly after beginning my new position closer to home, my hiring manager was transferred and her replacement demanded that I no longer work out of the office located 45 minutes from my home, but report to his office nearly two hours away by car—one way. Needless to say, I was beyond frustrated. In fact, every Monday I cried as I drove to work, commiserating over what a horrible mother I thought I was for spending so much time at work and away from my children.

As the end of every weekend approached, I was filled with angst, dreading my return and trying to convince my husband to let me quit. Much to my surprise, he would not. Months passed, and that became my pattern: appeal to my husband to let me quit on Sunday and cry for nearly two hours during the drive in on Monday. Then about nine months in, he suddenly agreed it was time to quit my job. Feeling liberated, that Monday morning I drove to work tear-free for the first time and marched directly into my manager's office and resigned.

Since that was just my second job following my college graduation just 14 months prior, imagine my surprise when the president of the firm called me into his office.

"Angela," he said, "we've been so impressed with your work we don't want you to leave." He continued, "What can we do to get you to stay?"

What followed served as another pivotal moment in my life and one of the greatest lessons I have learned about the power of resilience.

"I appreciate that," I responded. "But the only way I would consider staying is if you allow me to work from home."

Unfortunately he declined, citing they had never done that before and would not want to establish a precedent. I thanked him and respectfully returned to my desk to plan for my departure, but was soon interrupted by another request to return to his office. "Angela," he said, "we've never done this before but we're willing to give it a try for three months. Take the summer to work from home and hopefully at the end of the three months you'll consider returning to work here."

> Taking flight does not always mean flee—sometimes it is time to soar!

I am sure you get where I am heading. I did not return to that job at the end of the summer. Instead, I began my own firm with that top-ten public relations firm as my first client. The lesson: taking flight does not always mean flee—sometimes it is time to soar!

My first position after college was as associate director of public relations for The Corcoran Group, a luxury real estate firm in New York City founded and, at the time, run by Barbara Corcoran, now famous for her appearance on ABC's *Shark Tank*. During my brief stint there, I was privileged to join Barbara at the renowned Pierre Hotel for a Power Women Luncheon where she delivered the keynote address. She shared the story behind her coronation as the "queen of New York City real estate," recounting the days she faxed out one-page press releases titled "The State of New York City Real Estate" to media outlets from her one-woman operation in the living room of her home.

As a server belittled me for not knowing the difference between "real" tea and the Lipton tea bags that, until that moment, I understood to be real tea, three words traveled across the dais where Barbara stood to snatch me out of the past attempting to hold me hostage and elevate me to my future dreams: *perception is reality*.

Not long after the luncheon I was offered the position at the top-ten public relations firm. However, before I left The Corcoran Group, Barbara called me into her office and told me to write a vision for myself, challenging me to document where I saw myself in ten years. I am so grateful she did. I appreciate her push not only because I accomplished all of the goals I set for myself at that time, but because it taught me the power of casting vision, outlining my dreams and a plan of action to achieve them, believing those who refuse to dream choose to settle.

The Power of Living Life by Design

Perhaps a childhood peppered with a lot of moves makes it easier for me than most to embrace change. Maybe my disdain for monotony and interest in "what's next?" is spurred by my father's investment in my many adventures—summer camp, the Bahamas, Italy, Switzerland and France as a young girl—that opened my eyes to the idea that there is always more to see, learn and do.

This has served me well in my professional career, affording me diverse experiences as I moved from opportunity to opportunity, propelled by a desire to welcome new challenges, grow and live a life without limitations.

However, I have to admit I have this odd love-hate relationship with change. I have discovered I love and welcome change—as long as I control it! I love the freedom of my new, empty nest—until the silence speaks of the end of an era I can never relive. I love the spontaneity of a husband who enjoys splurging on a gift to surprise his bride—as long as it does not compromise the stability I enjoy when all of my bills are paid. I love the thought of a new job, project or challenge—until it tests my self-confidence and I am

How will we respond when the course to navigate to the change we want requires that we change?

wrestling with thoughts of inadequacy or fears of failure. I love the peace of obeying what I perceive to be the will of God for my life—until doubts arise attempting to question my faith.

I had a lot of experience with the latter in the past year, a time of truly transformative change marked by the end of familiarity and the beginning of journeys into uncharted territory in just about every area of my life. After a series of highs and lows, twists and turns—both good and bad—I have discovered the only variable I have control over is... me. This is where the proverbial "rubber meets the road." How will we respond when the course to navigate to the change we want requires that we change?

My 15-year career in public relations included eight as president of my own PR firm followed by six years in a senior management position at a highly regarded nonprofit. I enjoyed what many would describe as a dream career, an established reputation in my field, a cushy office, great benefits and a six-figure salary to top it off.

Yet I began to feel a familiar tug, that persistent prod when you know it is time to make a change. However, it was not simply a new project or a new job in the field of public relations; it was a call to go to work as executive director of community engagement and strategic partnerships on the staff of the church where my husband was founding pastor. Yes, my husband became my boss and began to sign the paycheck of the woman who once said, "I will never depend upon a man." Never say never! After some wrestling, I answered the call in some ways, returning to "the best of times and worst of times" as I walked away from the familiar and into the unknown. In doing so, I discovered that when being positioned for the change we both want and need, instead of looking ahead we begin to look back, fooled into believing where we were is better than where we are going. That, in essence, leads us into an insane cycle of pursuing what we want while wishing for what we had. The only way to break the cycle is to change our line of sight.

My work on behalf of A Woman's Business and as executive director of community engagement and strategic partnerships for Perfecting Ministries has allowed me to travel to some of the most challenged communities in the world in search of opportunities to be of service. Among them was the West Bank, that despite the negative perceptions of and the many problems plaguing the region —both real and manufactured—emerged as a place of personal discovery.

Traveling through various checkpoints that forced me to declare who I was and why I was there awakened in me a deeper sense of purpose and an unrelenting longing to not only unleash my potential, but the potential of all women. As I drove past the walls that divide mankind, I met some incredible women: *Christian women. Muslim women. Jewish women. White women. Black women. Hispanic women. Poor women. Educated women. Professional women. Unemployed women. Young women. Old women. Women who were mothers, daughters, sisters, aunts, grandmothers and trailblazers, such as Bethlehem's first female mayor, Vera Baboun.*

Regardless of our struggles and the differences that attempt to divide us, we all have one thing in common: we are resilient! When we fully embrace this reality, we will awaken to the realization that the "checkpoints" in our lives cannot limit us, as by nature we are problem solvers, able to skillfully weave something out of nothing, turning some of the greatest obstacles into world-changing opportunities.

Whether you are struggling with leaving an abusive relationship, giving up what others would define as the "dream job" to pursue your own dreams, transitioning from work to home or home to work, starting over or letting go, do not be afraid of change. The truth is change is the difference between where we are right now and where we want to be. I do not know about you, but I think it is about time we blaze new trails instead of retreating because we are afraid of getting burned.

> The truth is change is the difference between where we are right now and where we want to be.

Pursue Resilience

- Resilience is the ability to bounce back from adversity, allowing the obstacles in our lives to reveal who we really are instead of conforming us into who we are not.
- Face fears instead of running from them, as what we fear and avoid the most can lead to the most rewarding experiences in our lives.
- The "I will never" areas in our lives are where our fears reside.

- Remember those who fear vulnerability and risk never reach their full potential.
- The rigid break. Women are the "ribs," strong enough to hold up and resilient enough to flex, adapt, cover and protect what is most vulnerable and vital.

Living Life by Design

- Do not get so caught up in "doing" that you neglect "being" and never discover the real you. How you respond to adversity defines you, not your accomplishments.
- Know when to hold on and when to let go, understanding that flight does not always mean flee.
- Embrace change, realizing it is the difference between where you are and where you want to be.
- Know who you are. Perception is reality, shaping how you see and relate to others and how they see and relate to you.
- Your eyes *and* feet take you where you want to go. Write a vision for yourself and a plan of action to actualize it, remembering those who refuse to dream choose to settle.

Works Cited

[1]**Charles Dickens: A Tale of Two Cities, 1859**. First edition, Source: https://en.wikiquote.org/wiki/A_Tale_of_Two_Cities

Angela M. Brown is a woman recognized for making a difference and inspiring others to do the same. A seasoned businesswoman, Angela enjoys nearly 20 years of experience as a public relations executive, including eight years as president of OmniMedia Consulting Group, an award-winning PR firm she founded that specialized in media relations, event planning and media training.

Currently, Angela serves as the executive director of community engagement and strategic partnerships at Perfecting Ministries. She is responsible for communicating and executing the vision and mission of Perfecting Ministries and its affiliates through oversight of all marketing communication, media, government and community outreach, as well as identifying opportunities for community service and strategic partnerships, both locally and abroad.

Proud mother of KJ and Olivia, Angela passionately serves alongside her husband Kevin, founding pastor of The Perfecting Church, and oversees A Woman's Business, an international outreach to restore the purpose, power and position of women.

She uses her experiences as a platform to motivate women to turn obstacles into opportunities through frequent speaking engagements, mentoring, media interviews and as guest host of "Joy in Our Town," WGTW-TV.

Angela attended Hampton University and graduated from Rowan University with a bachelor's degree in Communication and a certificate in African American Studies. Her memberships include The Links, Inc., the Winslow Township Economic Development Council, the City of Philadelphia Mayor's Commission on Aging and the Urban Affairs Coalition Community & Economic Development Committee where she co-chairs the Employer-Assisted Housing Program subcommittee.

Connect with Angela at www.awomansbusiness.org.

TWO

OVERCOMING WORKPLACE BULLYING
BY ANGELINE LAWRENCE

Defining Resilience

Resilience is one's ability to adjust to extreme adversity without losing her sense of purpose and identity. Resilient leaders actually thrive in the face of opposition, because they are able to make adjustments to the changes they observe in their environment and counteract the attacks with skill and finesse.

My Story

I began my career as an urban planner working for a women-owned consulting firm in the private sector. Surrounded by caring mentors and a company leader who encouraged me to stretch beyond my boundaries, I felt I was ready to make a move.

Unbeknownst to me, working in the public sector in local government would be more challenging than meeting rigorous deadlines and being creative with my project approach for a client. As an urban planner, I left the private sector to learn the regulations and approval processes for development projects from the perspective of city government.

Helping communities rebuild their neighborhoods was a passion for me, but I needed to understand how government worked. The public sector, I soon found out, was laden with workers who were entrenched in the departments they worked for and had etched out unseen lines of demarcation that any newbie dare not cross. Several employees held vital institutional knowledge of the department because they had worked there for decades and constantly reminded everyone of their importance.

Add a bright-eyed, hardworking, young professional to the mix and you have a recipe for workplace bullying. My first project with one of those "old heads" of the department was a disaster. My colleague was much older and opposed to trying new approaches. We were tasked with the analysis of a dilapidated neighborhood area in the city that was once slated for a major commercial development. The development was never implemented so we had to provide a report of the current conditions.

Over the course of 18 months, I put up with his yelling and unwillingness to take my input on the project. We could only write one report, which meant I had to work with him to finish it. He refused to incorporate my edits into the report and bad-mouthed me to my supervisors. It resulted in several meetings with our supervisors trying to get us on the same page.

I lived through a textbook case of workplace bullying. Known as the silent epidemic, 65 million American workers are affected by bullying on the job. The Workplace Bullying Institute (WBI) defines it as the repeated, health-harming mistreatment of one or more persons (the targets) by one or more perpetrators. It involves verbal abuse, humiliation, threating and intimidating behavior, as well as work interference and sabotage[1].

My greatest mistake was not listening to my inner voice. In the early stages of the bullying, my intuition led me to talk with the supervisors and disclose the difficulties I was having with my coworker. Instead, I tried to work through it on my own. I opened myself up to him and tried to reason with him. In the private sector, I was trained to be a team player and we did not go outside of our team to handle disputes. We dealt with them among ourselves and found resolutions. Oftentimes, it made us a better team when we worked as one.

My greatest mistake was not listening to my inner voice.

Well, the rules were much different in the public sector and I failed to make the adjustment. Most of the employees worked as individuals and looked out for their own self-interests. Moreover, my coworker was known to be a difficult employee and had a history of not being able to work with others. I did not realize it until it was too late.

After months of trying to work with him I finally lost my composure. I was 7 ½ months pregnant and tired of being bullied. We had a deadline for a draft of our report, so I submitted my portion and added his. He accused me of changing his report, which I had not done. I went on a rant and released all the pent-up anger and frustration I had been carrying around for months.

Everyone's jaws just dropped, because I was the reserved one in the office. I had had enough, but allowing my emotions to overtake me only caused me further harm. I was slapped with the label of having an anger problem and my supervisors required me to take an anger management class. The confrontation was deemed the "Smack Down" by others in the office and was a running joke for years. I would look back at it and laugh later, however, it was no laughing matter for me at the time.

My supervisors started a file on me and documented everything that happened. I was the victim, was I not? I sure thought so. Playing the victim was my next mistake, as I realized no one wanted to help a victim. It was easier to stay on the side of the bully, a veteran employee who had decades on the job, as opposed to the new hire in the office.

The WBI refers to individuals who are bullied on their jobs as targets and not victims. According to the 2014 survey by WBI, 57% of targets are women, while 69% of perpetrators (bullies) are men. Targets are seen as threats to their bullies and possess more technical skills and abilities. They are independent and have empathy for their bullies.[2]

Yes, I was a target for bullying, but I did not remain a helpless individual looking for someone to defend me. I embraced healthy and faith-based strategies to combat the bullying I faced. In turn, I developed leadership skills, because my strategies helped me work with difficult individuals without being emotional. I was able to address matters in the office in front of the staff without sounding like a victim or forcing people to take a side. My leadership abilities improved because I grew as an individual first, by assessing my own characteristics.

I embraced healthy and faith-based strategies to combat the bullying I faced.

Recognizing and Removing the Enemies of Resilience

Being labeled with an anger management problem was a wake-up call for me. Instead of fighting the requirement, I took the class and changed my outlook on the situation. I shifted my way of thinking from being a victim to being an overcomer. I refused to stay in the negative mindset of blaming others for my unhappiness.

I rejected the label of having an anger problem. On the contrary, I looked toward my belief system to make positive changes in my life. I examined myself and realized I was not the individual others wanted to make me out to be; I was a hard worker and a good person. I did not let that event become the defining moment of me or my career. To continue in my passion as an urban planner I had to demonstrate my ability to work with others instead of being labeled.

Additionally, I vowed not to adopt the abusive behavior of my bully in order to survive. I had to stay true to my own personality and grow as an individual in order to be a leader. I did not undermine other coworkers. Instead, I continued to help others on the job and focused on the areas I needed to improve within myself. For that reason, I was able to work with difficult people without being overly emotional. I was determined to be a change agent by not perpetuating the culture of bullying.

I understood that I needed to grow stronger from this situation. We will constantly have to work with difficult people. However, as leaders, we must learn to deal with the adversity without it changing the core of who we are and blocking ourselves from our life mission.

Self-evaluation was a major step for me toward overcoming workplace bullying. I wrote down characteristics I felt I needed to improve. I measured myself against the characteristics of my faith in God, such as patience and forgiveness. Over the course of a month, I reviewed my list, checked off the areas I had improved in and added new areas I believed needed to be strengthened.

> I wrote down characteristics I felt I needed to improve.

Furthermore, I fed my mind and spirit with materials to help me become stronger in my faith. I read books on prayer and personal growth, seeking information and learning new techniques from successful business and spiritual leaders. Reading the stories of others who underwent challenging situations increased my confidence. I realized I was not alone and that many successful leaders also endured hardships. If they could make it through their ordeals, I could survive mine.

My next step was to confess my feelings of hurt, shame and embarrassment. I used the power of meditation and prayer to my God to help me through the situation. The five-minute confession allowed me to expel all the emotions and feelings I carried. As an effective leader, you must be objective and have the ability to think clearly. Purging myself of the toxic thoughts freed my spirit and cleared my mind so I could move forward.

Subsequently, I learned to forgive the individuals who I felt mistreated me. I suffered from a lot of hurtful actions by others, but forgiveness was my key to healing. My faith teaches me to forgive others so that I will be forgiven when I offend someone. Some call it karma, but it is a basic principle that what you put out into the universe you will get back. If I wanted forgiveness I needed to forgive others.

Reflecting on old offenses tainted my ability to be objective. I did not want to be defensive and pessimistic. Forgiveness enabled me to maintain a high level of professionalism that was devoid of unnecessary emotions. As a result, I had peace of mind and a calmness that helped me overcome future adversity. I gained stability and strength that helped me maneuver around difficult people.

If you keep the person hostage in your heart, you are harboring negative energy.

Practicing forgiveness also frees your spirit of the anger and hurt from the trials you withstood. If you keep the person hostage in your heart, you are harboring negative energy. Eventually, you will be upset and not remember what you are upset about. Forgiveness releases you from the evil intentions of the individual, so when you recall the circumstances they no longer have an impact on you.

Trusting my instincts was another important survival skill I had to master. In the beginning of the bullying, I should have followed my intuition. I was new to the office, thus using my sixth sense to navigate through the staff was crucial to my success on the job. I sensed something was amiss but ignored it. I learned to listen to my instincts for guidance by scheduling time for prayer and meditation every day. Reflecting on the events of the day was beneficial and helped me study my habits and make adjustments where needed. When we are leaders, being able to recharge our minds is essential to our success.

Those introspective moments were also my times of intimacy with my Creator. Dr. Maya Angelou's last social media post stated, "Listen to yourself, and in that quietude you might hear the voice of God."[3] She was correct, because it helped me stay aligned to my inner voice and listen to my intuition. Our spirits are very powerful if we relax and learn to take heed to warnings and the "warm fuzzies," as I call them, to avoid disaster or position ourselves for opportunities.

During my quiet time I expressed my gratitude for the love of God shown toward me. I delighted in my Creator by singing songs and doing happy dances. As I rejoiced in the love of my Creator my inner spirit became stronger. You cannot be easily broken down by the negative words of a workplace bully when you have a strong spirit.

Lastly, communication, both written and verbal, was an area I targeted after that incident. Learning how to speak up for myself without being out of control and overly emotional was pivotal to my growth. I developed a daily routine that included praying and meditating, confessing my feelings, continually forgiving others and maintaining a joyful disposition by singing and dancing (during private time) to my Creator.

This practice caused me to be more professional by detaching my emotions from the conflict or issue. I realized I had to get thicker skin and not take things personally. That way I did not jump into defense mode, but could observe the situation more objectively and respond with a solution quickly.

I established the habit of documenting every instance of a conflict with a coworker. My journal had notes including the date, the issue and whether or not the matter was resolved. I printed out any emails I felt were important and kept them separate from my work materials, never storing them in my office.

The experts and former targets of workplace bullying all provide the same advice—document, document, document. I followed those suggestions and copied my supervisors on emails with unresolved matters and provided a summary of the conversations when necessary. Additionally, I documented conversations between coworkers by following up with an email that stated the date, the nature of the conversation along with the next steps that were agreed upon to resolve the matter.

Many advisers caution targets of workplace bullying against approaching the Human Resources (HR) department. There is no law prohibiting workplace bullying in the United States, so the HR department would not have a point of reference to help targets. Furthermore, most HR departments are trained to protect the employer as opposed to the employee (WBI, 2014).

You should always document the first occurrence—and all instances—of workplace bullying by putting it in writing to your supervisors. It is essential to establish a paper trail, and in the event you decide to pursue a legal course of action you have proof that your immediate supervisors were aware of the hostile conditions you were working under.

Consistently include the date, the issue and a summary of what occurred. Do not include how it made you feel and what you were thinking. Keep it factual to what transpired. Addressing little conflicts in the beginning by documenting them helped me to deter any further occurrences. Once bullies realize you will not be intimidated and are organized they back down, at least for the moment.

Turning Reactions into Resilience

Years after the Smack Down episode I dealt with workplace bullying on a higher level in the same department. The former supervisors retired and the department had a new management team. I truly believed that a new culture would be instituted.
Unfortunately, the old ways returned with new players and higher stakes.

Under the previous management, the department was known for its high level of work and excellence. The legislative body preferred our division to review resident grievances and provide recommendations on major developments.

During the transition of new leadership the office was unraveling. The management team was overreaching into staff assignments and did not properly manage the department. On several occasions, I handed in my reports before the deadline, but they were misplaced or submitted late with errors. Likewise, crucial work requests assigned by our governing body were either overlooked or just lost on the desk of management.

I directly encountered work interference and sabotage as the supervisors overstepped their boundaries and actually performed the work that was a major part of my job responsibilities. Instead of doing my job, I was given busy work, such as photocopying and unnecessary clerical tasks. It was insulting and humiliating to have a master's degree and years of experience in urban planning, and be treated like a high school intern.

The environment in the office was hostile and tense. Other female staff members were enduring the same challenges, but no one would address it during our staff meetings. The breaking point for me was the day I received an email my supervisor sent to another planner from an outside agency. He copied me on the email. Once again, management missed a crucial work request, but the supervisor put the blame on me and stated that I was given the assignment.

This time I followed my instincts to speak up for myself and bring the issues of mismanagement before the staff.

The supervisor did not tell the truth because I had not received the assignment. I did not respond to the email, but printed it out and kept it. I took it to the top supervisor, informed him of what occurred and was told that it would be addressed during the next staff meeting.

The next morning during my quiet time I meditated on everything that was transpiring in the office. I sought guidance from my Creator, because I knew if I spoke up against this new team I could easily be fired. This time I followed my instincts to speak up for myself and bring the issues of mismanagement before the staff. The bullying was in a different form, nonetheless it was bullying and had to be stopped.

Our staff meeting was that afternoon. Once all the main items were addressed I raised my hand to be added to the agenda under comments. The top supervisor glossed over the issue of work requests and reports that were missed or submitted late with the old "we will do better next time" line.

I waited patiently for him to recognize me. My heart was beating out of my suit. Slowly and deliberately, I recounted the email message and stated, "Outside emails blaming staff for management mistakes is not right. I never received the assignment." I was led to continue, and addressed the fact that the system for work requests was a good one if utilized, but management seemed to be overstepping boundaries by doing staff work and assigning menial tasks outside of our job descriptions.

As I spoke, I felt 10 feet tall, although I only stand at 5 feet, 2 ½ inches. I was calm, my voice level was even, and I was in control of every word as I spoke with the authority my Creator gave me. I felt as if my Creator were speaking through me to bring light to the problems that had to change.

Once I finished, I looked around the table and other staff members jumped right in and voiced their concerns. My colleagues revealed that not only were some of the female staff members targeted, but a few of the male staffers were experiencing the same problems. We were able to dialogue in a constructive way and management realized they needed to make changes.

Surprisingly, I was approached by the very individual who bullied me when I first started with the department. He said, "Angeline, thank you for speaking up. I have been really going through with the supervisors. They were requiring me to copy land use maps and do a bunch of busy work. I was just being hounded. Thank you."

He left me speechless. Of course I told him it was no problem and remained humble, but I was absolutely floored. Due to my hard work and discipline, I was transformed and used by my Creator to speak out for others as well as for myself. Your enemies will eventually become a stepping stone if you believe in yourself to make positive changes.

Your enemies will eventually become a stepping stone if you believe in yourself to make positive changes.

The Power of Living by Design

Workplace bullying was a catalyst that helped me become a passionate and effective leader. I learned to draw my strength from my Creator and trust my own instincts as opposed to looking for the approval of others.

Utilizing tools such as meditation, confession and forgiveness on a daily basis keeps your mind and spirit clear of toxic thoughts. Yes, you will still encounter abusive people, but as you confess, forgive and meditate you will be free to respond positively. In addition, people will receive your words because they will sense your motives are from a pure place. No one wants to be associated with the office complainer. Their motives are self-centered and judgmental. They do not understand how to be objective and state their claims in an effective manner.

Resilient leaders can take a hit to the chin and stand strong while delivering a round-house punch. In other words, they can counter an attack with a concise response that is built on facts and not opinions.

> Resilient leaders can take a hit to the chin and stand strong while delivering a round-house punch.

Keeping my mind and spirit free from negativity helped me stay connected with my inner spirit. I drew from a well of strength and rejoiced in the love of my Creator. My process empowered me to find inner peace and a joy that was not based on status or material things. Consequently, I had the liberty to speak up when necessary because I did not have to appease the boss or seek to be in the office clique. I remained objective and cranked out high-quality work.

Because of my transformation, I defended my department to a real estate developer. Yes, yet again, my Creator used me to bring light to a situation. I was the lead planner on a mixed-use development project. One of the developers was pushing the department for an approval before we completed the review process.

I had developed a habit of saving emails and following up a conversation in writing, so when the developer questioned the timeline for the approval process, I responded in an email and provided the specifics of the review. Halfway into the process, the department was accused of not being forthcoming with a timeline, and the real estate developer was in danger of missing a critical funding deadline.

I was able to produce the email with the date and an outline of the process, showing that the person was fully aware of the time required to complete the review. That proof quieted the developer and we were able to move forward. Ironically, one of the supervisors complimented me and stated, "I am glad Angeline is on our team."

Pursue Resilience

Living your life according to your true purpose in the face of great adversity is the embodiment of resilience. Will you have setbacks? Yes. Will you make mistakes? Of course. The way you respond to the obstacle is what determines who you are. Allowing one incident to define who you are is unacceptable. Do what is necessary to overcome the setback. Look deep within yourself and never allow anyone else to define you. Follow these strategies:

- Self-evaluation is crucial to personal growth. It is easy to sit back and point out the shortcomings of others. Maturity is when you can reflect on your own characteristics and take steps to make positive changes.

- Make sure to set aside time for meditation and reflection. It allows you to reenergize and strategize for the day. You are then free to reconnect to your intuition. Most issues cannot be handled by a textbook method; you must utilize your knowledge and your instinct.

- Express feelings of disappointment and pain when you are attacked by confessing them out loud to your Creator. You will detox your mind and spirit and let go of the negative energy instead of continually replaying and internalizing the situation.

- Practice forgiveness because it frees you from being bitter. Forgiving your bully helps you heal. It does not matter if you receive an apology. Release the bully from the offense. If we want to be forgiven for our wrongdoings then we should forgive. We will receive from the universe what was in turn sent out into the universe.

- Be a life learner. Regularly seek out new information and resources that will help you grow professionally and personally. Empower yourself to be innovative and bring a fresh perspective to any project.
- Maintain good habits of documentation and follow up conversations in writing. You should always have a paper trail of what you do regardless of the industry or where you work.

Living Life by Design

As I live by the design of inner peace, joy and advocacy, I am continually honored by those who were my opposition in the past. Being a resilient leader helped me reach individual goals. Intentional living is the secret to success and overcoming obstacles.

- Position yourself to be a change agent and the "go-to" person to make things happen.
- Apply the skills you already possess and those you hone over time to propel yourself toward—and past—your goals.
- Get involved in your community. Collaborate with other like-minded individuals and commit to using your talents to train those who come after you.

- Tell your story! You can help someone else on their journey by sharing your own experience.
- Continue to maintain your inner peace and joy with daily quiet time and forgiving others on a consistent basis. Challenges will arise and you must maintain your composure as you enter influential circles.

Works Cited

[1]**Workplace Bullying Institute (2014**). 2014 WBI U.S. workplace bullying survey [PDF]. Source: http://workplacebullying.org/multi/pdf/2014-Survey-Flyer-B.pdf

[2]**Ibid**

[3]**Angelou, M. [MayaAngelou]. (2014, May 23).** Listen to yourself and in that quietude you might hear the voice of God. [Tweet] from https://twitter.com/DrMayaAngelou/status/469911477500272642

Helping others is a part of the DNA of **Angeline Lawrence**. A 20 year seasoned urban planner, she exudes a passion for helping residents and developers rebuild Detroit, realizing more had to be done. Angeline developed a micro loan program on behalf of the City Council that provided loans and training for Detroit-based existing and startup companies and served on the loan review committee for the Detroit Micro-Loan Enterprise Fund. Seeing the void of resources for aspiring entrepreneurs, she founded EntrepreneurExchangeGroup.com, a business blog for helping others find means to start their own businesses. Paradoxically, the widely publicized bankruptcy of Detroit led to Angeline's downsizing from her long time position, thrusting her into her own entrepreneurial path. She used her experiences to launch a consulting firm that provides industry development and administrative support to small businesses.

Angeline currently serves as the Chairperson for the Enterprise Entrepreneurship Institute (E2i) program, a new state-wide training initiative of the Michigan Black Chamber of Commerce, the largest in the country. Through her *Shine and Grind* podcasts, she provides Christian insight to women leaders of faith in the marketplace at ShineandGrind.net.

Her soon to be released first book, *The Working Women's Guide to Winning: Defeat Satan at His Own Game with Integrity* chronicles her story as a workplace bullying target. Angeline holds a bachelor's in economics and is a master's in urban planning.

Contact her at angeline@shineandgrind.net.

THREE

EXPECT THE BEST IN YOUR LIFE
BY DENISE G.HANNEY

Defining Resilience

I find myself occasionally sitting quietly in meditation, playfully connecting the dots backward to how I was led to this point in my life. Even with pain and disappointments my human side wishes I could have avoided, my spirit appreciates it all.

My faith and perseverance, rising above the naysaying and always keeping love first have created the woman I am now.

Always expecting the best in my life has and will continue to be my definition of resilience.

My Story

It never ceases to amaze me how elated I become when I wake in the morning, take my first breath and become aware of life. I am the mother of three beautiful women, grandmother of eight and great-grandmother of a lovely little girl. I have a life partner in a wonderful man and I serve as the CEO and founder of a company that is blessed beyond measure. Although I do not dwell in the rearview mirror of my life, I do choose to occasionally take a glimpse of what was, using that as a catalyst to gratefully propel forward.

Growing up in a brownstone located in Bed-Sty (short for Bedford Stuyvesant), Brooklyn, N.Y., with my mom, dad, maternal grandmother and my younger sister was a fun and comforting experience. That I had loving, working parents who provided shelter, food and clothing was evident and appreciated. Nevertheless, there was something missing, something vital. As a 10 or 11-year-old, I was unable to identify just what that was. While I adored my sister, who was 5½ years my junior, I would later identify my feelings as loneliness and uncertainty. Even though I enjoyed playing alone in my room with my dolls—my favorite activity—assuring each one that they had a specific task as I paid them with play money, I felt uneasy.

I would later identify my feelings as loneliness and uncertainty.

There was another factor in my life that contributed to this loneliness and uncertainty: the actions of my "Monday-Thursday-Dr. Jekyll/Friday-Saturday-Mr. Hyde" dad, my early introduction to the effects of alcoholism. As much as I tried to convince myself that my father's disease that created embarrassing situations of indecent behaviors did not bother me, it was years later that I witnessed how my choices were a result of how I felt about his behavior, but mostly, about myself. Let me take a breath and digress.

At the age of 12, I was visiting my friend down the block where we were avid double-dutch jumpers. After a long day of jumping and while retreating to dinner, she asked, "Did you have a twin brother?" I am sure I looked at her as though she had three heads when I replied, "No!" She again proceeded to explain how her mother told her that I had a twin brother or sister. As gossip was the "thing" on Lefferts Place, I bid her goodnight and hurriedly walked home. Wanting so much to share what was mentioned by my friend with my mom, imagine my surprise when she asked me to sit down so she could explain.

My mother, ever so quietly and with slight evidence of sorrow, disclosed the existence of my twin sister, Diane Grace, who passed away 30 days after her birth due to an enlarged heart. She also explained how she was afraid to discuss it with me because I was such a strangely sensitive child. She further revealed I named most of my dolls Diana and, in my younger years prior to the birth of my sibling, Linda, would speak to an imaginary entity during the day or while at play. This answered so many questions, one of which was the loneliness I felt in a room full of people and my passion to feel the comfort of a partner.

The old adage "looking for love in all the wrong places" seemed to have developed into my life road map. Confusing love with sex, attending events and places where I know my angels protected me, and failed relationships were products of this

The old adage "looking for love in all the wrong places" seemed to have developed into my life road map.

mapping. All the while, I considered myself a productive and giving lover of God, a well-behaved contributor to the human race.

After marriage to a man whom I cared about but truly used as an instrument to get out of my functioning, yet dysfunctional household, my eyes were opened wide on the day of the wedding. I witnessed his definite love of alcohol and drugs (I bet you saw that coming). Within a 12-year period I raised three children almost as a single parent while married, moved from residence to residence due to lack of funds and support, and was constantly emotionally and physically abused. During this time of good, old-fashioned survival, it was revealed spiritually and through an *Oprah* show that I could do bad all by myself.

Twelve years of that nightmare navigated me toward my journey as a single mother, separated from my husband along with a plethora of life epiphanies. Reinventing my life at the age of 35 was not my original plan.

I worked in corporate America for 20-plus years and thought I planned well for a wonderful husband, children, a home with a pool, a dog and a cat. I lived in America, and I wanted and planned for the so-called "American Dream." My maternal grandmother would share a cliché that I did not quite understand until my plans started to crumble: "Man appoints and God disappoints." I just saw it as my grandmother's interpretation of God's disposition that to me was mean and unfair.

I spent Sunday after Sunday during my youth in the Church of the Nazarene and St. Phillips Episcopal Church in Brooklyn, N.Y., and even a quaint gathering at Saturday School. Despite the time I invested, it was rarely discussed how much God truly loved me and how I would have the ability to create the life I desired through faith. Even if it was mentioned, the do's and don'ts and consequences leading to a permanent residence in hell was more prevalent. It was not until TV ministry became my visit to church on Sunday. In my late 30's I realized our Creator was close and reachable and I could have a personal relationship with the One who made me.

I was even more excited when I learned that I did not have to be proficient in the old King's English to speak with Him. Thee, thou and any word that ended with "eth" needed not be uttered from my lips. What a relief! Knowing I could touch my Creator and speak with myself, reveal my heart and seek guidance without feeling judgment allowed me to surrender fearlessly. Passing this new wisdom on to my children so they would not have to suffer as I did was still more exciting.

Even with this wisdom I acquired, I realized I was not living; I was just existing. I walked numbly through the motions of motherhood and occasional dating not feeling life. I was still seeking and wanting, but I did not know how to accomplish anything. This was the beginning of not only recognizing who I was, but of placing life in perspective as it pertained to being the "authentic me" and ridding my mind of demons that prevented me from living the best life possible.

As I worked daily on living these revelations, I was consistently and diligently met with what I was feverishly running from. It was as though an email blast was sent out to the world of negativity stating, "Denise is finding her strength and purpose. Let us place any and all obstacles in front of her to prohibit this."

Hindrances like saving money. This was a struggle when my car broke down on the highway or when the father of my children found every excuse not to send money to provide for their basic needs. The financial issues spiraled into an emotional depression that I dared not share with anyone so I could maintain my "I'm Every

Woman" status. Almost every life choice, every endeavor to create a business or to rectify any emotional or financial issue that was created either by myself, my ex-husband or whatever life, I believed, was throwing at me, was met with some form of failure.

Recognizing and Removing the Enemies of Resilience

With all that I endured, I knew it would eventually affect not only my performance at work but, most importantly, it would not serve as an example for my children. That was equally as important to me. I truly recognized the following enemies that were hindering my overall success in life:

1. Negative or unsupportive voices from outsiders.
2. The occasional internal voice that insisted I was not good enough or a non-essential to give advice to or partner with, personally and professionally.
3. Concerns of financial lack and the inability to create a doable financial plan.
4. Not fully exercising my faith in God.

Why in the world was it so important for me to receive approval from anyone in my life to pursue what I knew was right for me? Why did I internalize, analyze and eventually allow anyone or anything spin me into a deep sadness, trying to pull myself together while masking it with false happiness and people pleasing? Why was I entertaining thoughts of suicide? SUICIDE? That was when I knew my story had to change.

On a sunny, beautiful, autumn afternoon, while my daughters were in school, I decided to take a half day off and go to the one place that always brought me joy—the beach. I have a choice of beaches to visit, I thought, while driving on the Southern State Parkway in Long Island, N.Y. I asked God to place me where I needed to be. I was led to my favorite place, Robert Moses State Park in Suffolk County, N.Y. I parked in the lot with a view of the Atlantic Ocean meeting a clear, blue sky. Since pen on paper was always my comfort zone in communicating, I decided to practice an instrument I heard of called deliberate writing. You write your thoughts and ask the question(s) and answers will or can be revealed if you surrender your mind, heart and hand to your writings.

I decided to practice an instrument I heard of called deliberate writing.

Honest and revealing everything in my heart—loss, hurt, gratefulness, confusion, love, discomfort, failures and desires—I spoke to God with words on paper. If vocal, it would have sounded like run-on sentences with no breath taken. As I came to the end of my writings, my hand loosened and began to have a life of its own. Love, peace, joy, comfort and hope filled my spirit and two pages, reassuring me that if I stayed in faith, built a personal relationship with my Creator and continued to be the "best Denise" I could be, the desires of my heart would be fulfilled. What was fascinating was the handwriting was not mine. It was a much larger script, loose and free-flowing. It was not structured, even or on the ruled paper the way I was taught in elementary school.

Taking what I experienced very seriously, I tucked the writings in my bag and made the decision to be the best Denise I could be and expect the greatest life for myself despite the unwanted ranting of the external and internal voices of woe. Within weeks, this incident was followed by vivid dreams and visions of one who expressed love, several children in my presence, a beautiful home and women asking for and being provided with food and money. I now understand that these dreams and visions were prophetic.

Turning Reactions into Resilience

The true friendship of women is a glorious and powerful force. While in the midst of taking care of family, friends and being involved in community matters, my girlfriends presented me with a gift of pampering at a day spa. After my massage, facial, manicure and pedicure, I left the spa in a levitated state as I drove home. Everything was so clear for the following two weeks. I immediately came to the conclusion that every woman and man should feel this way. I felt so empowered. I was less tired, able to accomplish projects with ease and give my family and myself the attention needed.

Realizing that opening up my own day spa with only $25 in my checking account after mortgage payments and my daughter's college tuition was an impossibility, I sought the demographics of the areas I was interested in targeting. God placed in my heart to create a mobile spa for those who were unable to afford the high prices of a day spa, those who were shut-in and those who may have had child or adult care issues. It was also available for men and women whose schedule did not permit time for what I considered to be a mandatory health and wellness service.

In 2001, The Spa Expectations Corporation/Expectations Mobile Spa & Women's Resource Service was created. This became my passion. I woke up and fell asleep with thoughts of how my colleagues, my support system and I could best serve individuals, families and communities. Bringing spa and quality-of-life services to my family and friends was ideal as a trial run. Making business and personal errors was less painful when done within the realms of family and friends who loved and cared for me, thus giving me the confidence to pursue a larger and extended audience.

Needless to say, through this endeavor I was visited by the negative voices: "Why would you want to waste your time?" or "Girl, you will never make any money doing this." Even though I am sure those who called themselves giving me sound advice may have been doing it because they were concerned and meant well, every fiber of my being pushed me to fight the naysaying and follow my dream and what I knew was my calling.

Every fiber of my being pushed me to fight the naysaying and follow my dream and what I knew was my calling.

Funding also became an issue. Lack of funds due to being a single parent, maintaining a household and trying to create a business without seeking the instruction needed also became a stumbling block. I spent many evenings after everyone went to bed and early mornings before everyone arose searching the Web for information on how to start a business and reviewing grant opportunities for small businesses. *Starting a Small Business for Dummies* became my friend; we were joined at the proverbial hip.

Keeping in mind my experience at the beach with the deliberate writings, and once again recognizing the demons that made themselves quite evident through the naysayers and my internal bickering, I did the following:

1. Blocked the negativity through meditation and prayer.
2. Included time management to assure a great quality of life for myself and my children.
3. Enhanced The Spa Expectations Corporation with events, parties and offering services, despite a lack of funds. I made sure I acquired financial stability through deposits and full payments, allowing me to purchase what was needed, pay contractors and enhance the business with baby steps.
4. Faced problematic issues head-on with a positive perspective.

Through those actions and through connections via those steps I was placed in a position to acquire corporate and private clientele. It seemed as though my dream and what my mother saw in me when I was a child came to fruition—I became a philanthropist and the CEO of a company.

THE POWER OF LIVING LIFE BY DESIGN

I now live on purpose. This phrase echoes in my mind from a very inspiring quote I heard Yolanda Adams (gospel singer and motivational speaker) profess at the end of her radio show, "Live On Purpose!" I have learned to be conscious each and every moment throughout the day. I capture and hold each of these moments by acknowledging the beauty in and around me. Every tree, every child, every breath I take, and the joy I feel each time my husband enters the room becomes a testament of how much I appreciate my life and what the universe is offering. As a result, I never have room to entertain any destructive thoughts, whether from others or from myself.

This realization has been the foundation of the continued success of my business. The same clarity I experienced when I was gifted with my first spa treatment is now an everyday occurrence that allows me to effectively communicate, create and implement the services I hold so dear to my heart. On a personal level, the same holds true. Communicating, creating situations and discussions without being offended or feeling judged, and bringing what I envision to light is a feat I thought would never come to pass.

One of the games I loved to play with my mom was Connect the Dots. It was a cute, strategic game that involved a grid of dots. I would connect two dots and then my mom would connect two dots. The first person to complete a box placed her initial within the box and gained a point. Another Connect the Dots game that was interesting was the formation of an object or dots that led to something wonderful like a pot of gold or safety out of the forest.

God is undeniably the Great Dot Connector in my life and the lives of men and women with whom I have had the pleasure of sharing my experiences. Each moment, incident, adventure and venture—good and not so comfortable—led me to the life that I love today.

During the spa's inception, I juggled raising three lovely girls, taking care of a home and maintaining employment to fund The Spa Expectations Corporation and deal with the powers-that-be. There were never any regrets. The passion that was placed on my spirit was so great that working a 12 to 15 hour day was a blessing—even at times when falling asleep writing a proposal, producing a radio show or designing a set to create a spa-like venue became commonplace.

Various religious and business texts affirm that faith without works is dead. Although I deem my Creator the Great Connector of dots, nothing can be gained by just sitting back and letting life do its will. The key factor here, and another spiritual and secular business belief, is if you want something, you must visualize it. Do as much work or research as necessary, acquire connections through networking and most of all, act as though you already have it. The blessings in my life have been nothing short of a miracle and evidence of divine intervention and being consistent and focused with the steps I mentioned.

...nothing can be gained by just sitting back and letting life do its will.

As a result of living by design, I accomplished the following:

- Creating a successful company that is dear to my heart where I have the privilege of serving and empowering others.
- Maintaining successful personal and business connections—more than I can count or mention.
- Meeting my husband, who is also my best friend.
- Acquiring my lovely home in North Carolina.
- Becoming a proud grandmother of eight healthy and beautiful grandchildren and great-grandmother of one.

Pursue Resilience

Within this journey I learned so many things about myself, about adversity and how it affects me as well as how to rise above it. I have trained my mind, body, soul and spirit to pursue resilience:

- The time is now! I adopted that thought with the understanding that there will never be a perfect situation to start a project, a business or anything worthwhile. I realized that if I waited to have enough money, lose enough weight, until the children were older, etc., my vision would never be achieved.
- Nothing is beyond my reach. I can do all things through strength from my Creator.
- When the external and internal voices bombard me with negativity, I find a quiet place to pray and meditate, asking the universe to remove the harmful voices and bless me with affirmations, eliminating the "middle man" who tends to create havoc—myself.

Living Life by Design

- Awaken each morning with a prayer, a smile and gratitude no matter how you feel. Happiness is a choice! Embrace the day with declarations of "I will have an amazing, happy and successful day and nothing or no one will stand in my way!"
- Despite what negative feelings may have been self-engrained in your mind, know that you are a beautiful, loving, gifted woman who is wonderfully made by God.
- Surround yourself with individuals who are of like mind and those who have or are heading toward success in their personal and professional lives.
- Love is first and foremost. Love is the key to holding on to your resilient nature. You should have love for yourself, your family and friends as well as those whom you deem "the enemy." It is also essential to express love for the universe and the wonderful gifts and wisdom that are constant in your life.

Denise G. Hanney, a woman of God, partner to an amazing and loving husband, mother of three beautiful adult women, grandmother of eight healthy and blessed individuals and great-grandmother of one precious great granddaughter, also holds the position of CEO and Founder of The Spa Expectations Corporation and Expect-ations Mobile Spa & Women's Resource Service currently serving communities in New York, New Jersey, Connecticut, Virginia, North Carolina, Florida, Illinois and California.

Her love of nature and relaxation is evident by her multi-faceted establishments that cater to women and their families in promoting self-esteem, self-worth and self-care through self-awareness and pampering.

Because she governs her belief in love conquers all, Denise's ministry far exceeds merely pampering. She wraps her passion around consulting on 'quality of life matters' such as health, wellness, nutrition, family entertainment, career, entrepreneurship and also home decoration on a shoe-string budget.

Denise inspires you to open your mind, to awaken to your self-empowerment, to recognize you are more than enough in accomplishing anything you choose and most of all to live her signature mantra, *Expect the Best In YOUR Life!* ™

Meet Denise at TheSpaExpectationsCorporation.org.

FOUR

LIBERATING YOUR TRUE SELF—AT ANY AGE
BY DIANE BLAKE

Defining Resilience

You can spend a lifetime living someone else's version of who you truly are and never know it. You may have worked in careers that were professionally satisfying racking up awards, promotions, great salaries and the high regard of colleagues and friends who comprise the critical audience in your life. Still, despite your successful career performance, deep within can lay a nagging sense you are neglecting something, as if you took off on a month-long vacation and forgot to water one of the plants. all.

That feeling recurred many times throughout my working life but I pushed through it. Not until a few years ago did I decide to examine what the nagging feeling was about. Discovering that changed me. I recognized there actually had been a plant I failed to water most of my life—me. Fortunately, I also discovered I was one of those resilient, strong-rooted plants that bounce back from long droughts and still thrive. You may be among the many women who are as well.

Are you priding yourself on multitasking in the endless corners of your professional, social and private life with the last disappointment or setback serving as the foundation to move forward? While hiding your true self is not astoundingly dramatic in the eyes of others, it is devastating nonetheless. To be your true self, you have to push past the pain, hurt and fear. You must become a survivor. You do not have to go through tragedy in order to have challenges. Living is a challenge. Life happens and yet it is not the challenges that make you; it is how you deal with them.

Judging by what they saw on the outside, many people said I appeared perfectly suited to the career labels I wore. They commented on how pulled together I looked, projecting a kind of credibility and outward confidence that proved to be a magnet for both promotions and romantic dates. Many successes were achieved as a lawyer adjudicating administrative hearings, teaching law, serving as an assistant commissioner of a government agency, sitting on the board of directors of a citywide bar association, and acting as chairperson of a not-for-profit corporation, all while enjoying the challenge and prestige of my career.

Inside though, I felt like an impostor with the jobs and career serving as a mask. While succeeding in numerous positions, there was still a strong sense in my spirit of leaving something behind or leaving something important undone.

If you are known as one of the baby boomers—as I am—you may be like that. You may be among the "first achievers." A lot of "firsts" encountered the loneliness of leaving behind the familiar. One mental health expert I spoke to hypothesized that "baby boomers are particularly prone to this phenomenon of being the first" (J. Wade, personal communication, April 11, 2015). We were the first in our family to go to college, to move into desegregated housing, to enter office jobs in downtown corporations. During that time, the world was experiencing unprecedented expansion. Optimism was high. The sky was the limit — there was nothing that could not be achieved. That was the mindset during my formative years in elementary, junior high and high school.

As the first in my family to graduate from college, loneliness was a constant companion. Firsts generally moved away from the familiar into the unknown often with or without mentors. We prepared the way for others to follow, used what we had and invented our way to success. We became pioneers.

Resilience is part of the human experience. The world cannot advance without it. The early American settlers had it. My ancestors had it. I define resilience as the ability to adapt, change and use challenges as opportunities to re-invent ourselves. That is the brilliance of the baby boomers. We were the re-invention generation. We could always find ways to make things turn out for the best. Our actions were our self-proclaimed resilience, all the while rebounding with grace.

My Story

I started as a child with a low self-image, living life with the belief of not being good enough. But over time, I metamorphosed into the person I am today. With growth comes change. Through incremental baby steps, things are learned, created and forgotten. Mistakes are made and rebounds are responses to them. Reward comes from certain choices and criticism from other choices.

Falling in and out of love, marrying and divorcing are part of that life, a life of constant change for better or worse. Life always presents hidden blessings.

> Life always presents hidden blessings.

Growing up in Baltimore, Md., as the middle child of six children in a solidly working-middle-class family, my parents were great role models for a strong work ethic and for being a responsible citizen. There was no better family for me to grow up in. Ours was a close-knit, church-attending, loving family, with cousins as playmates and some of the best memories of Sunday dinners at my grandparents'. Life was grand. Then something happened on the way to living life.

More often than not, life choices are heavily influenced by family expectations, community habits, cultural practices, social norms and dramatic social change. Those influences can either curb potential or set it free. The childhood influences that shaped me did not have a law career in the picture. In fact, the vision was to graduate from high school, get married and get a job—any job so long as it paid money. Like everyone I knew, I did my best to comply.

In junior high school, one teacher noticed my academic strengths and suggested I attend the college-focused, all-girls high school on the other side of town. It meant applying to high school like I was going to college. I applied, was accepted and began a life-changing journey.

The students were different from me in how they thought about the world. They were college-bound children of upper-middle-class professional parents. Most were the daughters of teachers, principals, school administrators, nurses, doctors, lawyers and social workers. Their parents were also foreign to me from what I knew about people who worked.

They were sometimes called "uppity." By definition, I was considered middle class, growing up in a two-parent household where both parents worked, owned their home and drove a car. But college was not on the radar in the neighborhood I came from. Any expression of interest in upper-middle-class aspirations was met with the withering, "Oh, you are one of those uppity people," or a dismissive, "Stay in your place." It seems so strange talking about it so many decades removed but that was the way it was. Instead of making choices about what kind of life they would have, those I knew accepted whatever life handed them. Choosing was an unheard of concept. Dreams and desires did not exist based on what you could achieve, but rather what you already possessed.

In high school, I got swept along with new girlfriends in a new crowd. Besides having a different outlook on life, the other unusual thing about the group was that it was racially mixed. Plus, college was on the agenda for them. Their conversations were sprinkled with talk about their older siblings who attended the University of Pennsylvania, Princeton and Brown. Vacationing in Martha's Vineyard, travelling to Europe and dazzling those in earshot with their talk of shopping trips to Lord & Taylor's in New York City was par for the course for them. Their parents bought them cars. The mother of one classmate drove a blue four-door Jaguar. I decided I had to have one. It was the snazziest car I had ever seen. Their talk about life was new to me. Unlike where I came from, they acted as if they were in control of their futures, and I was a sponge soaking it all up as they taught me a lot about how other people lived.

Going to college as a full-time student and working a part-time night job at a bank, I had no social life, parties or fun times with classmates in the canteen. After class I rushed downtown to work from 3:00 p.m. to 11:00 p.m. Then it was home, read, eat and go to bed. That routine could have prompted dropping out or quitting. It would have demonstrated a lack of resilience rather than the better choice of rebounding and pushing on.

During college, being recruited along with a group of other students to intern as student teachers, I was full of glee when hearing about the program. It meant experiencing life in fantasyland —New York City. Although I did not know what I wanted to do in life, I knew teaching elementary school was not exactly it. Yet education was appealing so it was a matter of finding the right role. After graduation I landed a job as an editorial assistant at a magazine in New York City. That was my calling—loving words, reading, writing, speaking and teaching. The job was in a creative business environment whose main purpose was providing information to help others. That kind of teaching was it! But with no foundation for making my own decisions, it was easier to yield to the pressure of friends who said my teaching degree was being wasted.

It would have demonstrated a lack of resilience rather than the better choice of rebounding and pushing on.

Business and communications were as far removed from my background as folks back then who believed there would never be an African American first lady in the White House. Reluctantly, after two years, I gave up my magazine job and took the familiar path of most college-educated black women—teaching. I taught fifth grade for a short time and eventually got laid off along with hundreds of other teachers due to budget constraints. The students, the community and the colleagues were all great, but I desired a different option as an instructor.

After teaching elementary school, I worked in the political arena as a special assistant to the New York City public advocate, who was a female lawyer. As a consequence, going to law school was an easy choice to satisfy my desire to help others solve problems.

I found satisfaction for the great part of me that enjoyed research, reading and helping to settle issues. Still the nagging feeling of not experiencing my true self remained. The further I moved up in my career, the more the pesky emotion from hiding behind a mask and being a fraud persisted.

Recognizing and Removing the Enemies of Resilience

The breakthrough to my true self began comically only a few years ago at the shampoo bowl of a well-known Manhattan hairstylist. Some of the ladies were discussing weight, exercise and diet. Passing by, the owner chimed in, "It's not the weight; it's the big 'C.'" We laughed. He later explained that the big "C" was the inner confidence many people lacked and did not realize it. I did not give it much more thought.

The next day included attending a church reception to welcome our new pastor and his family. With a fresh hairstyle, manicure, designer suit and purse, and my signature red lipstick, I was very confident in presenting myself. However, the outer me was masking the transparent inner me. In a conversation, the pastor's wife said, "We would love to use you around here but you lack one thing: confidence."

Those words hit right in my spirit and nearly took my breath away. I knew God was speaking to me. Without getting defensive or angry, I thanked her and acted as if nothing happened, though so much had happened with just that one word. I felt oddly inspired when I arrived home and spent the entire night making a confidence board.

> I felt oddly inspired when I arrived home and spent the entire night making a confidence board.

I went through every magazine, cutting out words and pictures and put them on a corkboard in a place where I could easily see it every day and night. The energy came from a rushing fire within, going way beyond being tired the next day at work. The change was not immediate. Bit by bit, resilient step by resilient step, change happened and my self-confidence grew. Without role models on how to go about doing it, it was hit or miss and trial and error, me refusing to give up. I worked at excavating the true me night and day and adopted the attitude that small things matter. Slowly but surely, people began to see and comment on the change in my inner self. Nothing on the outside was changing. The inner me was moving forward and shining through.

During that process, one thing was certain: I had to take full and total responsibility for being at that point in my life. God showed how my thinking and believing got me there. The changes that needed to be made were also mine to make, without crying or feeling sorry for myself. A spiritual force propelled those shifts away from the excuses and blame bubble I created. Society, my background, lack of support or rejection were no longer "go to" excuses for not living out my God-ordained purpose with confidence. It was time to break all the self-imposed rules and take a deep dive.

> It was time to break all the self-imposed rules and take a deep dive.

On a core level, the question remained: Was I really as good as I thought I was? When coming from a false belief of "not good enough" it was easy to create stories to feel better, wearing fig leaves of achievements to cover those feelings of inadequacy. The more successful I was, the greater the feeling I had of being a fraud. The negative self-image had not changed. It was covered up by an unreal self-image that was not the truth. External successes were used to solve internal imaginary self-problems, a success-oriented approach to problem solving.

The success-oriented approach to problem solving goes like this: Will they approve of you now? Will they think you are good enough? That is the driving emotion. You strive for more and more in order to feel good enough. The more you get, the worse you feel. You believe you are a fraud, an imposter and undeserving, so you strive for more in order to feel good enough. It is never ending. There is always someone who can jump higher, run faster, sing better. At the intellectual level, you know no one is better than you. You understand you are different and do things differently. In your heart, however, you do not believe it to be the truth for you. You still want to be good enough.

All of those value descriptions are mental illusions. They are words on a paper. They have no value unto themselves. Certain kinds of green-colored paper and silver and tin coins have value because the United States government says they have value when, in fact, the paper is just paper and the coins are just coins until value is assigned to them.

Until you learn to value your contributions, you will likely cover up the feeling of "not good enough" with fig leaves and masks. You might spend enormous amounts of time and money on things to make you good enough. Along with that comes stressing out because of trying to please others—bosses, family and friends. Those external successes still do not bring the feeling of good enough. When you focus too hard on trying to measure up, you forget you are already adequate. That kind of self-focus becomes useless. It solves no problems. There is always a higher bar to reach.

> When you focus too hard on trying to measure up, you forget you are already adequate.

In my case, I developed hypertension and went to the hospital thinking I was having a heart attack. It was one whole night and day in the hospital, a day lost from work and my absence from an important event I promised to attend with someone. And all of that took place after having the "confidence" epiphany. Even while knowing what was wrong I did not know how to stop what had become my normal. It was time to figure out how to create a new normal.

Turning Reactions into Resilience

My "not good enough" influenced everything. From a very young age, I set out to prove to myself I was good enough, making choices based on how I wanted others to perceive me. I fought a private internal war because my outside did not match my inside. It was like twins fighting each other. They looked the same yet they were not the same. There was a mental illusion, an internal conversation of "If I am good enough to them, then I must be good enough; case closed." But the case remained opened.

As I began to like myself (building God-esteem), the blessings in my life became easier to see. I was a success and was already everything I wanted to be, had done what I wanted to do and possessed what I wanted to have. It became a matter of seeing it, believing it and acting like it. From there doors began to open that could not have been foreseen because the focus had been on the problem and not the solution.

As I began to like myself (building God-esteem), the blessings in my life became easier to see.

Being part of a women's leadership group for two years with women from across the nation who were leaders in ministry, not-for-profits, government and business was one example. Another example was taking a course at Harvard Law School and sitting in a class with leaders from all over the world, including a female prime minister of an African country. As iron sharpens iron, it was exhilarating to meet and know those people. To test my leadership skills, I became the president and chairperson of a not-for-profit corporation, learning it was possible to be feminine, professional and a leader.

At the same time, I spent one solid year studying and learning gratitude, learning how to be grateful for the little things as preparation for the big things and choosing to see the possibilities. Every day, I thanked God for allowing me to experience a day never before experienced. Each day was a found treasure to open up and see what was inside.

There was an opportunity to see firsthand how prevalent the thought of "I am not good enough" was in our "win-at-all-costs" society. While acting as a volunteer attorney with a women's law boot camp, another attorney and I provided feedback to a group of six young lawyers on an assignment they were previously given. Their goal was to argue and persuade us on the law and on their problem-solving skills. They were some of the smartest and brightest young lawyers, much like me. They were dressed in the lawyers' uniform of dark tailored suit, white shirt, high heels and styled hair, eager to learn, showing a readiness to hear and do what we had to say.

But something was missing. They were terribly insecure and unsure of themselves. Each person was very nervous when presenting and some asked for do-overs that were graciously given. Upon receiving the feedback, their responses were downcast looks and comments like, "These are not the things they teach us in school," "My boss doesn't help me with this," and "I don't have a mentor." After the general discussion with the entire group they asked if they were lawyer material. We said resoundingly, "Yes, you are, without a scintilla of a doubt, bona fide lawyer material," telling them to stay connected to their women's organizations.

The Power of Living Life by Design

Then an ah-ha moment came. That "not good enough" feeling I had been living with was a farce. Each person was different, from different backgrounds and cultures, trying to be the same by measuring against a standard that did not exist. Those young women had a life and career of stress and worry. There was a desire to ask them what would have been ideal to ask myself: "Who are you not good enough for and what is a 'good enough' person? What does she look like? How does she act? What makes her good enough? If you are not good enough, then what is the standard or criteria to be good enough? Please show it to me."

With this newfound awareness, my focus is now on mindfulness living. Some people call it living with intention and purpose. I focus on enjoying what I have and living to make a difference. There is no longer focus on self because all the self-talk is an idea, a thought or belief based on what I or someone else may think perfection should look like. And that belief is almost always based on comparing myself to something or someone else. There is now an acceptance that I am not perfect and do not have to be in order to measure up to my own or someone else's concept of me. I am who I am. You are who you are—created for a unique purpose.

Pursue Resilience

Pursuing resilience is a process that does not happen overnight. However, there are things you can do immediately to improve your everyday life. Here is what I did and what you can do too.

- **Master your mentality.** Changing childhood beliefs and cultural beliefs is not easy. Change takes time. So, what can you do in the meantime of waiting for change to happen? You can meditate on or imagine how you want to be, the kind of life you want to live and the change you want to see. It is a matter of life and death. Meditate means to mutter. Take quiet time to mutter within your spirit, mind and body about the results you want based on your thinking. This small change of mastering your mentality can make a huge difference in your daily life. Once your signature stands for who you really are, you will be a person of excellence and influence. People like associating with a winner and with people who make them feel like winners.

- **Exercise daily.** Of course the major benefit of exercise is fat loss. It can also increase lean muscle mass as well as raise a person's metabolic rate, or how fast a person burns calories. Being out of shape at any size is not healthy. Go for a toned, vibrant, healthy look instead of going for the skinny. Skinny does not look healthy on everybody.[1]

- **Develop a sleep routine**. Believe it or not, sleep is a physical activity. Ironically, it is one of the least appreciated activities in our fast-moving, get-it-in-a-nanosecond world. If you do not believe sleep is a physical activity, try staying awake for twenty-four or more hours and see if your body does not drop from exhaustion. Neither can you force yourself to go to sleep. Like relaxation and meditation, you have to let go and sleep. When you are sleep deprived, your body may become exhausted and your thinking, moods and behavior can be erratic and unreliable. You are then more susceptible to illnesses and possible overeating.[2]

- **Body by design: Eat healthy foods for your body type.** People come in all shapes and sizes. Your body is designed by God to restore and maintain health. It is not important if everyone is a size 6 or 8. What is important is living at your optimal health. A good diet coupled with nutrition is the way to stay healthy. Excessive anything is not good for the body. You are what you eat and you can eat anything in moderation and in variety.

- **Create a success image that is not performance or perfection based**. Live according to purpose. Purposeful living is mindful living. It means being aware of the now, what you are doing and when you are doing it. Like driving a car, one centimeter off thought can cause you or someone else her life. This will be a new approach to life and a new way of being. You have already been chosen for the success and achievement you desire. They are built inside of you. What may look like failure may be part of a divine plan to show what living the life you were created for looks like. In other words, show and tell. Living this way will make you smarter, prettier, richer and wiser. Your confidence will soar. Self-image based on authentic confidence will have a positive effect on your business, career, wealth, even how you treat others.

Living Life by Design

Our stories are written to encourage you to live life by design. The following is what I learned about this concept during my season of finding my true self.

- **Create a vision board** and place it where you have to see it daily. It really works! The vision board serves as a map that helps define your destination and reinforce the steps needed to get there.

- **Create a supportive environment** at home and work to engage your five senses with images, sounds, tastes, aromas and things touching your skin, making you smile inside or even laugh out loud.

- **Make a habit of stretching beyond your usual comfort zone** and be surprised at how it will gradually build your confidence and open your mind to possibilities you never imagined. Your experiences have value, so rock what you have to identify what you feel would be success in your life and develop the habits that will deliver this success.

Works Cited

[1]**Broer, T. (2004).** *Maximum fat loss*. Auburndale, FL: B&A Publications.

[2]**Kabat-Zinn, J. (2009).** *Full catastrophe living: Using the wisdom of your body and mind to face stress, pain and illness***.** New York, NY: Bantam Dell.

Diane Blake is an attorney, author and speaker. Having served on several boards, she has been blessed with a wide variety of life experiences from lawyer, assistant commissioner to college professor and entrepreneur.

Her heart's desire is to lead women to live remarkable lives with style, confidence, wisdom and grace. Her leadership, expertise and passion have been recognized by the prestigious Coro Foundation's Leadership Program in New York, and she was named one of the 25 Most Influential Women in Business by the Network Journal Magazine.

In keeping with the tradition of philanthropy, she believes each one, reach one. Because of her willingness to invest in others, she served as Chairperson of Footsteps to Follow (FTF,) a not-for-profit speakers' bureau devoted to career development in youth where she presently sits on the Board of Directors.

As founder and CEO of Step Right, Inc., Diane equips, encourages and empowers young people to make a difference by developing *leadership*, engaging in *service* and launching *change* in their communities. She motivates youth to see and execute possibilities they may not have otherwise known existed. More than ever, Diane knows kids need these three core philosophies to overcome the odds in an ever-changing world. Diane believes giving our youth a "right start" is not only the right thing to do, it is an essential "step in the right direction" to securing a bright future for us all. She is also an Adjunct Professor of Business Law and enjoys serving in the teaching ministry at her church.

Visit her at DianeBlake.com.

FIVE

Learning to Make Room for What is Best

BY FAYOLA DELICA

Defining Resilience

Various challenges early in my life have helped me understand and form my own definition of resilience. I was a people pleaser in my youth, probably because my mom was a people pleaser and consequently my siblings and I became people pleasers. Ironically, being a health care professional was no help in getting rid of this unhealthy mentality.

My life was put on hold to help others, thinking it was the Christian thing to do. After being alone and having to face the hardest, darkest and lowest moments in my life, my eyes have opened. I can no longer put my life on hold to help others live theirs. With no assistance from family or peers, resilience is what undeniably pushed me to knowing who I am, accepting who I am and living the true path to my authenticity.

Please know you need no one's approval or the permission to say yes to yourself, yes to life and yes to all the good and great things that being on this earth has to offer. Remain, as I have, centered on standing firm in your power and strength to reach your dreams and goals no matter what. That is resilience defined.

My Story

In moving forward, I am astonished to discover the worst thing one can face is refusing to reminisce or recall former challenges. No one wants to face the past and relive trauma. There are, of course, wisdom and insights to be learned from every experience. Never would I have guessed that meeting Dr. Deana Murphy in 2014 while we both waited for airport transportation in Atlanta would change my life. Who knew this chance meeting would lead me down this transparent, health-giving path of penning what I have aggressively tried to suppress.

Healing comes from forgetting the past, or so I thought. But the reality is I am now experiencing a true restorative journey in facing and sharing with you what I wanted to never think about again.

When speaking professionally, I tend to tell my story with an ease of not having to process the emotional connection that comes with writing it. In reading this, I ask that you be encouraged and choose the transparent path toward treating the bruises of your past.

The wall behind the smile

Since a little girl, I hid behind a protective wall in hopes of preventing people from getting close to me. At such a young age the smiling little girl carried very deep scars. Most of my life I was an extreme extrovert. However, I concealed the darkest part of my soul with all the pain and suffering I endured as far back as my memory would go.

One of my earliest, darkest memories was having the worst nightmares for many years. Because of the nightmares, I was afraid of death and darkness. I remember being in kindergarten hysterically crying with feelings of a dark spirit of death walking with me. I told my teacher I was afraid to die. She and my parents wondered why I was thinking of death. What caused me to think I would die?

That was just one of the challenges I faced early in life. Then as a young girl, on numerous occasions I was molested by several older men who were acquaintances or friends of the family. Most, if not all, were of Caribbean descent.

The most hurtful part of my story is that I expected my dad to protect his daughter. Even though I did not tell him about the violations until after I became an adult, I feared my father had let me down. I naively thought my father was that "all-knowing man" who could discern when his daughter was being taken advantage of.

Although my father said he was sorry for the heartless things that happened to me, I could not think of him as my dad. I felt he did not do his job in keeping me safe. In my understanding of fatherhood and because he was the first man I loved and trusted, I believed it was my father's responsibility to protect me. The lack of love and closeness with my father affected my relationships with men and the ability to trust people, especially men of Caribbean descent.

Prior to suffering through those incidents, I was considered a healthy child. But with those hurtful experiences at such a young age came various physical problems. At age five, while walking through the corridors of my school, I passed out. Since then I have dealt with epileptic seizures, vertigo, skin conditions, gastric difficulties, migraine headaches, childhood obesity and a scalp disorder. I visited different specialists and hospitals throughout my childhood but no one could find the cause of my ailments. As I got older, most of the conditions left on their own.

I always seemed to struggle with thoughts of life and death. It would have been cowardly easy to allow my early years to be reason to not fight back and just accept life through the lens of my pain. However, with my unshakable faith and unquestionable stubbornness, or should I say my firm persistence, earlier experiences allowed me to count it all as winning. How is this? I won because those battles allowed me to build inner strength with tenacity to set high personal standards and objectives. My belief is that I must have possessed an inner obligatory resilience, because to my knowledge I was the only one in my immediate family to have endured so much. Oddly enough, there is something deep down inside me that makes me feel I should not have made it to my 32nd birthday.

I won because those battles allowed me to build inner strength with tenacity to set high personal standards and objectives.

Then I grew up

Fast-forwarding to my adult years, I worked very hard to acquire two bachelor's degrees—one in Health Science Education (BSHSE) in 2003 from the University of Florida, graduating cum laude within three years; and a Nursing (BSN/RN) degree from the University of Miami in 2005.

With such academic accomplishments, God's blessings and hard work, I moved to Charlotte, N.C. in 2006 after completing a traveling nursing assignment for a male correctional facility in the southern part of Vermont. In 2007, a few months after moving to N.C., I built a four-bedroom home in the suburb of Matthews (right outside of Charlotte). I was a young, single, registered nurse in my early twenties who had attained my dream life! And I did it alone. I thought I had arrived. At the climax of my career and life, I was an active church member serving in various capacities and ministries, a full-time seminarian, politically active and a volunteer in my community.

The voice of warning

"Yes you are young with job security and living the good life, but get your financial house in order," I heard the still, small voice say. Then 2008 happened. Soon I discovered nothing was guaranteed to last forever.

An economic crash hit and I had nothing to fall back on. I lost everything. As a per diem nurse, my hours were reduced because of budget cutbacks. This affected my ability to meet my financial obligations and as a result, I began to experience extreme financial hardship. In addition, I had to stop going to school for two reasons. First, my seminary was located in a vastly conservative Republican area where I felt targeted as a very liberal Democrat. This became especially apparent after speaking in 2008 at the HR 676 (Single Payer Solution Bill) Caucus Reception at the Democratic National Convention in Denver, Colo. My second reason for not returning to school was because I was repeatedly sexually harassed by one of my professors.

To make matters worse, I lost someone very dear to me—my uncle. He was a Catholic priest who helped me understand who God is and what it meant to have a personal relationship with Jesus Christ. In remembering the injustice my uncle experienced from the Catholic Church and how he suffered at the hands of disloyal supporters in advocating for the poor and Caribbean immigrants in the United States, I was angered and torn by losing him. In addition, it made me question my faith, because how could God allow someone who sacrificed so much for the kingdom of God to die at the hands of his enemies?

Also during this time, with no warning, the relationship with my church in Charlotte was severed. I felt as though I was being shunned by my neighbors, and on top of all of that, my friendships and family relationships dissolved. I felt abandoned by everyone, even God. There was no one to call for help or to come alongside me and guide me in making sense of how to make it through.

At that point, I sensed betrayal by everyone. Being isolated from all that had given me joy, peace, security, purpose and meaning in life caused an emotional dive. My happy world had turned completely upside down in the blink of an eye.

I felt God had taken everything away from me, leaving only a miserable life. I hate to admit it, but there were many times I wished He had taken my life in all the mess. It was absolute torture to experience those hardships in such a short time span and to later feel the effects linger for so long after.

Recognizing and Removing the Enemies of Resilience

Everything in me was fighting against all that was happening to me. I was enemy number one. My perception was that I did not deserve all that was taking place for a number of reasons: a) I was a young, single black woman; b) I played life by the rules and was a law-abiding citizen; c) I was a devoted believer and follower of Jesus Christ and paid above my tithes and offerings with not just my money but with my talent and time; d) I gave to others when I did not have enough for myself; e) I opened my home twice to help people in need and they absolutely took advantage of my kindness; f) Did I not suffer enough as a child that I had to endure more pain and suffering as an adult?; g) I sacrificed a lot in life through community service. Did that not count in preventing difficulties from happening to me? I could go on and on as to why those things should not have happened to little ole me.

No matter how much I complained, pouted and cried, the worse things seemed to be. I had no control at all. The more I tried to save myself, the more out of control things became. Slipping into depression, my personality and thinking began to change. I did not want to believe in God anymore.

Enter enemy number two. I stopped praying, reading my Bible and worshipping because I believed those things did not matter nor appear to help me. I had suffered enough as a child and had finally received a break in my 20-something life, or so I thought. Constantly asking myself if God was real, I began to question everything I knew and believed.

The more I wanted to give up on my faith, the more my deeper core would pull me back to God. Once I awakened His truth, I removed the self-inflicted, self-destructive attitudes of anger and bitterness and began looking internally deeper to change my perspective on what was taking place in my life. I made the quality decision to own and activate the power I possessed. When we are meant for more, we have to peel off the layers of what has been placed on us to find our true selves, our true path.

I made the quality decision to own and activate the power I possessed.

Turning Reactions Into Resilience

Five years had passed. It was time to close the pity party, pain, suffering, blame and unforgiveness chapter to open a new one.

I knew my life would never be as it was before 2008. Changing everything about me without forgetting who I was and all that I had been through was my goal. I had to modify how it impacted me. Going through pain and suffering was one thing, but having to revisit those dark moments to gain the pearls of wisdom that were obtained along the way took courage, maturity and strength.

Even while penning my experiences I hesitated to share the dark moments because I was afraid of reliving the mental and emotional torment. However, I am now able to see my true self, my inner strength as well as the need to change how I defined my value and identity. I had to break away from using possessions, education, accomplishments, associations and occupation to describe who I was. I learned to express myself by who God created me to be. I made room for what was best. I was a natural leader—from a girl scout for over a decade to various leadership hats I wore in school, in the community and at church.

I made room for what was best.

I knew greatness was in me, but identifying it was the challenge I faced before I could share my gift with others. Many great leaders had to endure so much hell before they were able to see their leadership gift blossom for a greater cause than the pain and suffering. That gave me a better understanding of resilience. There is a difference between merely being resilient and living life by design through the power of resilience.

The Power of Living Life by Design

There is a certain poise about one who is called to be a leader; the greatness on the inside seamlessly makes its way to the outside. However, it seems before one reaches this enlightenment a number of hardships are endured in the process. I believe the power of living life by design is one of the rewards in enduring the difficult times in life. It is not something you can learn in a book or acquire through traditional schooling. Trust me, I have tried. Through life's experiences you will rightly understand your personal level of resilience and inner power—the backbone for living on your own terms. Living life by design defines that power. Those terms are not based on what society or others determine for you.

On a personal note, I have rechanneled the pain and suffering that gives me insight into my significance in life. I am a survivor. I do not believe God allowed me to weather the storms only to live in mediocrity. There is a lesson in every encounter. Being determined to go after my goals no matter how hard or how long it takes is how I choose to live by design. This approach also encourages me to reflect on the lives of biblical characters and my role models—the great leaders who went through hell before arriving at their destined place. As a diamond is just a rock before it is refined and purified, I believe we are much the same.

Being determined to go after my goals no matter how hard or how long it takes is how I choose to live by design.

My people-pleasing days are over. I discovered how to live on my own terms and not worry about how it may affect others. You have to develop tough skin in the process of becoming resilient. You must then formulate a survivor's plan to withstand all that will come against your inner strength, not backing down but pushing forward in reaching your goals by being all you were meant to be.

Settling or accepting the status quo is not an option. I do not believe my losses were in vain. Hopefully, with extreme gratitude and appreciation, the generations in my bloodline will see me as that positive role model because of my sacrifices, courage and resilience, just like I do for my dear maternal uncle, maternal grandmother and the many others who came before me.

The purpose in sharing my story is to help you bounce back from suffering real pain when life hits hard. Adversities are not stop signs but detours to finding your true path and purpose. Be encouraged to stay strong and draw your resilience blueprint by reflecting on the strategies below.

Pursue Resilience

- Regarding your finances, prepare for the challenges you may face ahead. Be conservative in the good times by having something stored up for those rainy days. Times like these will undoubtedly come.
- Along with an emergency fund account, gird yourself with whatever keeps you grounded. For me, it was from a spiritual standpoint. I strengthened my intimate relationship with my God through reading the Bible and praying to learn how to weather the storm with peace. I came to trust that "this too shall pass" (ref. 2 Corinthians 4: 17-18, *NIV*) and "In all things God works for the good of those who love him, who have been called according to his purpose" (ref. Romans 8:28, *NIV*).

- Getting to know yourself in a deeper way must be an ongoing part of life's journey. In finding your authentic self a better outlook will emerge regardless of challenges you have overcome, are facing now or may face in the future. You will be strengthened. After going through the worst time in my life, I took an introspective approach. In doing so I now realize that life is an opportunity to dig deeper in understanding and valuing my inner strength. Once you spend time in self-discovery, each obstacle then creates opportunity to become pliable in every area of life. I believe this point develops true resiliency in the high-potential leader. In the words of Shakespeare, "Know thyself."

- Never give up, no matter what comes. I know you have heard this many times and you must continue hearing it. It is one thing to have an intention or a dream, but it is imperative to deliberately plan how to achieve that vision. The most inspiring leaders I have met or read about overcame a number of setbacks while building tenacity to persevere. Thus, whatever your aspirations, a well-defined strategy will keep you grounded with a burning purpose when faced with devastating circumstances.

Living Life by Design

- When you are bouncing back from the low places in life, it is hard to regain your confidence. A suggestion to rebuilding your confidence and self-esteem is to surround yourself with people who will help you as you strive to reach your goals and dreams and who will celebrate your success. In addition, you want to associate with like-minded people who are optimistic and positive. The more you hang around negative and pessimistic people, the longer it will take you to recover.

- In finding a reason to enjoy life again, reconnect with your goals and dreams, no matter how old they are. The real dreams that are a part of your purpose in life will never die. They find a way to resurface. Be sensitive and aware of the recurrent themes that identify with your goals and dreams. In doing so, you will find your true self and peace. There is something about living a purposeful life that makes sense when looking back on your past. You begin to see your pain and suffering as part of your process.

- Whatever goal you have in mind, set a strategic plan for how you will reach it. You may have to make a number of changes. It starts there. Forgive yourself for all you have been through. Write your story to get healing from your past, then find a way to share it with others. The more you keep it to yourself, the more the pain will linger and give power to those who have hurt you.

- Create a 'before' and 'after' collage of who you are and where you want to be. This will allow you to see the growth and change you are seeking. As you do so, celebrate every small step toward your objective. Each victory will encourage you to continue moving forward as well as help you pace your progress in the process of reaching your desired end.

- Do not allow the hardships in life to keep you locked up. Release the restraints in your life by living life by design. You have the power and ability to be that high-level leader.

Fayola Delica, a native of South Florida, is an author, professional motivational speaker, life and business coach and talk show host. She is the founder of Fayola Delica, LLC., a professional motivational speaking and life coaching services company assisting individuals in setting goals, strategizing a plan to reach them and managing the careers and businesses of speakers.

Fayola founded The 360 Evolution Academy, a holistic etiquette school to feed her desire to pour into the lives of others, especially the youth because so many people have poured into her. Her weekly "Finding Your Hidden Treasure" BlogTalkRadio show discusses issues related to business, entrepreneurship, youth, leadership, and Christians in the marketplace.

Recently appointed UNA-Southeast FL Human Rights Day 2015 Chair, Communications Chair and to the Broward County Human Rights Advisory Board, Fayola is passionate about advocacy and human rights. She was formally trained as a health educator and registered nurse. She is an award-winning member of Toastmasters International and volunteers as an iCon consultant for Junior Achievement (JA) of South Florida, Inc.

She has authored two e-books, *The Ultimate Speaker's Manual: The "How To" In Presenting a Professional Speaking Business* released October 2014, and *The Ultimate Life Coach's Manual: The "How To" In Presenting a Professional Life Coaching Business*, released May 2015. Visit her at www.FayolaDelica.com.

SIX

A SALUTE TO SUCCESS—
THREE PRINCIPLES TO OVERCOMING OBSTACLES
BY GLENDA O. COOK

Defining Resilience

"Life is what happens to you while you're busy making other plans"
- John Lennon

Life happens. Whether we are prepared for it or not, it happens. Oftentimes we find ourselves questioning why it is happening to us. The answer always lies in the obstacle. It just depends on whether or not we are prepared to pull up our bootstraps to stomp over it. Resilience is just that—the ability to tighten your bootstraps with a willingness to fight when the terrain gets rough. It is your disposition to resist the authority, force or obstacle defeating you. Being a resilient woman is daring defiance! It requires you to defy the odds. No one would have ever expected what was about to happen to me. I certainly did not expect it for myself.

My Story

It all started on a beautiful, clear day in December, a month full of joy and holiday cheer. The weather was as perfect as could be for winter. It was Florida, after all. Cool, yet sunny and I had just returned home after a long, life-altering day. Still in disbelief, I plopped on the couch in my empty apartment. My body was heavy, as if I had bricks weighted on each limb; I was numb. My heart sank deep in my chest as my mind raced. The first tear fell from my eye. I was in shock and could not hold it in any longer. I felt defeated.

All day I went through the motions and followed my routine, hoping no one would notice. I hid behind my smile, my lipstick and my stilettos, staying engrossed in my daily tasks. It was not joy behind my smile, however, it was sorrow masked into a package that women design to give the illusion of everything being intact. There I was hiding behind the same mask, behind the camouflage of a smile, pretending nothing was wrong. Hiding was an outlet for me. It allowed me the time I needed to accept what was really happening while I was in denial.

There I was hiding behind the same mask, behind the camouflage of a smile, pretending nothing was wrong.

In my mind, December became a season of apprehension and gloom because I had a secret. It was a secret that would not be kept for very long, as the truth would come to light in less than a year. It affected my ability to fulfill my dreams and changed my life forever. However, I was determined to not let it get in the way of the whole reason I was in Florida in the first place.

Being the daughter of two military parents taught me how to be self-sufficient and resilient. I learned leadership at a young age, and I knew I was destined to lead in one of the most dynamic organizations ever. I was four months into a three-year contract that would allow me to pay for school and commission as an officer in the United States Army. This was a task that less than 1% of Americans achieved. I strived to be included in that 1%.

My secret—I was pregnant. Nineteen years old and pregnant, to be exact. How could this have happened to me? I mean, I was an honor roll student athlete, an avid volunteer in the community, my high school senior class president and vice president of the student leader organization. All my life, I tried to prove societal statistics did not apply to me. I had my life all mapped out.

Immediately, I went through a guilt trip, blaming everyone but myself for what happened. Truthfully, there was nobody else to blame. I was in this predicament because I made a bad decision. There I was, a scholarship student almost a thousand miles away from home at Florida A&M University (FAMU) with a guaranteed job upon graduation, falling to societal statistics. I was petrified and furious with myself, but I could not show it. There was a strong disconnect between who I wanted to become and who I had to pretend to be because of a bad decision. It was then I realized I had to make one of the biggest decisions of my life.

Recognizing and Removing the Enemies of Resilience

There will constantly be a defiler or detractor ready to block your rebound. Defilers and detractors can be people, places, things or issues. Some may call defilers "haters" or "blessing blockers," while detractors can include relationships, money and health problems. In other words, they are all enemies of resilience that can hinder your decision to be defiant in the face of adversity. But remember, these enemies are put in your life for a reason. You just have to find out why.

I faced an enemy of resilience as soon as I set my plan in motion to succeed despite my current setback. I drove to the Reserved Officers Training Corps (ROTC) building on campus to ensure I would not lose my scholarship. I had to meet with my ROTC instructor immediately. He was slightly intimidating. When you visualize an Army soldier as depicted in movies, you think of him—large, muscular build and ready to take on the world. He was a Master Sergeant, one of the most senior ranks you can acquire on the enlisted side.

Although embarrassed, I had to inform him, as my due date was around the start of the new school year. I needed to take a leave of absence in order to stay on track for my scholarship. I rushed to my instructor's office, gently knocked on the door and asked to speak to him in private. "Sure. Close the door behind you," he said. As I turned to close it, I took a deep breath and put on my artificial mask to give him the news.

"Master Sergeant," I said, "I am pregnant." It felt as if I just dropped a bomb on his desk. My words felt so heavy and everything seemed to stand still around me. Expecting a supportive answer, I hung on to his blank stare and heavy sigh, yet he said nothing. He just looked at me perplexed. Nevertheless, I continued because I felt the need to convince him. "I need to take off the fall semester because I am due to have my baby in August. I will be back the next semester." Still he said nothing.

Finally, his mouth opened to comment. It felt like minutes had passed until the first word was spoken. "Glenda, be honest, you are not coming back."

Who was he to tell me what I was and was not going to do? Although annoyed by his statement, I attempted to demonstrate restraint and respect with my reply. "Excuse me, Master Sergeant?"

"You are not coming back. Statistics show that most women who get pregnant in college do not return to finish. I think it would be easier for you to drop out and go back home to Virginia."

As my heart beat faster and faster, I felt my body temperature rise. Not only was I disgusted by his response, I was enraged! I could not believe the words coming out of his mouth and I started to sob uncontrollably.

"Just drop out and be more realistic about your situation. You are not meant to be an officer in the Army. You will not survive it," he said.

I think my gasket blew! I could no longer hold my restraint. That man was supposed to be my instructor, my leader, my role model! Instead of motivating me, he discouraged me by predicting I would fail. Maybe he misunderstood the strength of a woman. Doubt was simply fuel and it was all I needed to spark my fire. I looked him square in the eyes and said, "I will be back, and I will graduate no matter what you think. Watch me!" I stormed out of his office, rushed down the stairs and crashed through the front doors for fresh air. I felt like the walls were closing in on me.

Maybe he misunderstood the strength of a woman.

Outside the door, my ROTC commander noticed the tears rolling down my face. Seriously concerned, he asked why I was crying. I barely got the words out, but somehow he was able to interpret what just transpired as I gasped for air between phrases and tears. "Do not worry about it," he replied. "You will be fine." As much as I believed that, it was helpful to hear it from someone else.

> As women, we constantly try to validate our worthiness, intelligence, ability and equality.

Society had me believe I would not persevere because most give up. That is what people expect and that is why we are always trying to prove otherwise. As women, we constantly try to validate our worthiness, intelligence, ability and equality. We should not have to, because we are all of those things and more. Just look at our body of armor! Recognizing this helped me realize I was my biggest enemy to resiliency—not society or my instructor for that matter, but me. When I first found out I was pregnant, I doubted my ability to even keep the baby. My thoughts were disheartening. No one could say anything to me or about me that I probably had not thought of already. I thought my instructor was right in a sense. The odds were against me. I was unmarried, unemployed, had less than $2,000 in my bank account and no family around to help. Then I realized it was "little me" whispering. "Little me" is the voice in the back of your head that tells you to give up. It is the voice chiming in when the light bulb comes on with a bright idea, telling you not to bring it up. Your thoughts are your biggest enemy! Recognize there is power in your thoughts and that positive thinking produces positive outcomes.

Turning Reactions into Resilience

The world breaks everyone, and afterwards, some are strong at the broken places. - Ernest Hemingway

Have you ever dreamt of what life would look like in the future? I did. I would get my education, start a successful career, get married, have kids and maybe sprinkle in a dog or two—the all-American Dream. However, things do not always work the way we plan, now do they? The reason is because we are not in full control.

Being pregnant at that stage in my life was definitely not in my plan and was out of order. We cannot always choose the order of our steps and must understand this concept to grasp why we are constantly going through storms. That was a lesson I learned quickly on this journey we call life. After having such a setback and my instructor attempting to foretell my future, I could have given up, as statistics have shown many to do, but I did not have to.

I control my destiny, not my enemies! How do we take the hand dealt to us and transition it into a successful outcome? Embrace it, learn from it and drive on, that is how. The obstacle does not define you, what you do next does. You have three choices: give up, give in or give it your all to succeed! Giving up and giving in were just not a part of my DNA. I had the audacity to believe all things were possible. In order to do that, I knew I had to believe giving my all was the only choice.

> Every great leader has a test before she can lead through her testimony.

There the mission began. I started to transition my mind from thoughts of defeat and self-doubt to thoughts of dreams and self-confidence. Although it was not on my terms, I discovered the lesson I was to learn from the experience. As a leader, you are faced with many obstacles you must overcome and this was my first test to leadership. Every great leader has a test before she can lead through her testimony.

I discovered my secret was not a burden, but a blessing, and having a can-do attitude was just what I needed to take me over the hump. I had to defy not only my instructor, but the negative voice in my head in order to succeed.

The Power of Living Life by Design

There is a personal responsibility in taking command of your life while seizing the moments intentionally designed for you. In order to start creating a plan of action, you must rebuke all negative thoughts. I did just that as I strategized my return. First, I listed everything I needed to accomplish. It was somewhat of a checklist where each item or goal listed was Specific, Measurable, Attainable, Realistic and Time-bound, or S.M.A.R.T. Whether a goal is attainable is up to interpretation, considering your enemies believe it is not. Just remember the only interpretation that matters is yours.

For each action item, I applied a simple formula to ensure it was checked off my list: *determination*, *dedication* and *discipline*. Here is how it played out: I did take the fall semester off from school to deliver a baby boy. While out on a leave of absence, I worked out several times a week to stay in shape. I created a budget to itemize all my new expenses, allowing me to get a better understanding of what I needed to survive financially without any assistance. I took the lessons I learned in an investment course and started investing the $2,000 in my bank account to increase my emergency fund. I searched for affordable townhomes and resources available to me, like hand-me-down outfits for my son, to limit expenses. The non-profit where I volunteered had a program to help women with children go to school, so my selfless service paid off immensely.

With a plan of action, I was able to return to FAMU the following semester with my son in tow as I said I would. These are all examples of my *determination.*

Can you guess the first place I stopped once school started? My ROTC building was at the top of my list. I walked through the halls with my head held high, proud of what I was able to achieve. I was back! Heads turned, as nobody could believe that I returned to school in Florida when I could have easily transferred to a school in Virginia. I went straight to my ROTC instructor's office to inform him I was back, only to learn he had moved overseas to finish up his military career. It did not matter because I had a plan.

At the crack of dawn, I drove clear across town to drop my son off at a home daycare in order to make ROTC training three times per week. I sacrificed my social life to stay on track with my studies and new motherly duties. Every once in a while, you have to evaluate what is keeping you away from completing a task and eliminate it. That was not easy for me, but the easy way is not always the best solution. I had to put in the time necessary to keep up my grades for my scholarship. My *dedication* to achieving my goals did not allow me to get derailed.

Every once in a while, you have to evaluate what is keeping you away from completing a task and eliminate it.

Ensuring an on-time graduation, I took 21 credit hours, three semesters straight for a bachelor's degree in business with a minor in military science. Would you believe I earned straight A's the first time I attempted it? My grades were better as I released negative thoughts and focused on positive outcomes. It turned out my new blessing kept me in check. I was able to manage my studies, go to physical training and raise my son, all by myself. Only with *discipline* was I able to accomplish this.

Now you may say, "She is a soldier so it is easier to have a defiant warrior mentality." That is the wrong answer. This formula is designed for all women, because we are all warriors destined to lead, whether in our homes or in business. The ability to balance life, love, family and our career is profound. Our *dedication* to our families is why we make it a priority to attend our child's practice or concert and still fix dinner after a long day at work. Our *determination* to be successful on the job is why we are able to get promoted or land that new gig. Our *discipline* in money management is why we are able to look fabulous, maintain a home and still take that relaxing vacation. We are already living warrior lives by design, but we must recognize it first before others can acknowledge it.

I knew what I was able to achieve, but it was natural for me to still wonder if anyone else knew. I got my answer the day of graduation. The time had finally come, and my family was present to see me commission as a second lieutenant in the Army. My son was there too, smiling at what his mommy was able to accomplish. He did not know at the time, but he was truly my motivation. I wanted to prove it to him more than anyone else.

There will always be that one person who secretly doubts your abilities or openly gives you an unwanted opinion.

As I stood on the stage all dressed in my uniform, I could not help but remember the time when that man told me to quit and I was not going to make it. Has anyone ever told you to give up? Were you told something you tried was not going to be successful? You are not alone. There will always be that one person who secretly doubts your abilities or openly gives you an unwanted opinion.

Keep in mind just because they say it does not make it true.

It was my turn to take the oath of office, confirming my commission as a leader in the military. After it was all over, I looked up and there was one person who made everything around me stand still—my old ROTC commander. Although he had already retired, he came back to see us graduate.

"Lieutenant Oakley, take this business card." I gazed down and noticed it was not his card; the name belonged to someone else. Puzzled, I looked back up at him and tears filled my eyes. He remembered! Not only did he recall the tears he saw after my instructor told me to quit, he never forgot the flames in my eyes when I returned to school with my son. "Call him and tell him," he whispered. "Tell him that you did not drop out. Tell him that what he thought of you was incorrect." His voice raised with each declaration. "Tell him to call you ma'am because you now outrank him! Call him. Call and tell him to salute you because you did, in fact, make it!"

I was so overwhelmed with emotions. A sigh of relief came over me and I felt redeemed! Finally.

Although it was befitting of a junior officer to render a salute first, my commander locked his heels and slowly raised his hand to salute me as I stood in shock! You see, the salute is not simply an honor exchanged. It is a privileged gesture of respect and trust among soldiers. It is also recognition of each other's commitment and abilities. This salute meant so much more. It was an expression that recognized the personal commitment of my sacrifice—my sacrifice to lead. I smiled at the sheer thought of it all. Joy was now present in my smile. I no longer felt defeated; I felt hopeful. Quickly returning the gesture to him, I stood in my power, the power of knowing I controlled my destiny and what others thought of me did not really matter.

We have the ability to alter the outcomes in our lives if we are willing to work for it. How you take a setback and turn it into a setup for your next stage in life starts with shifting your mindset. You see, life happens in seasons, and seasons bring changes of weather. There will be days full of sunshine and days that are cloudy. You will experience moments that jolt you like lightening or frighten you like thunder. Every once in a while a storm will brew, but the rain cannot last forever.

We have the ability to alter the outcomes in our lives if we are willing to work for it.

Adversity is an opportunity for growth, and that is exactly what I did. I grew to be relentless and fearless and discovered more about myself than any class could have ever taught me. I went from questioning my resiliency to leading 100 soldiers in Iraq at the age of 23. Three years later, I acquired my MBA. The discipline learned from tight money management techniques allowed me to be the owner of two homes with a significant investment portfolio by the age of 30. I successfully transitioned to corporate America, started my own consulting business, and my son is a thriving, intelligent student athlete, musician and future author.

My story of triumph does not mean there were not days when I wanted to give in. My *determination*, *dedication* and *discipline* just would not let me.

When that moment of doubt strikes you, ask yourself these questions:

1. What would happen if I did not give up?
2. What would happen if I did succeed?

Realizing it was not about me helped. It was all about him—my son.

3. So, who will motivate you to stay on track and finish the mission?
4. What will help you elevate your setback to a resilient setup?

Live on purpose and do not let anything get in your way. Be a defiant leader and rock your salute—you have earned it!

Pursue Resilience

- Realize there is power in your thoughts, so shift your mindset to positivity.
- Understand the obstacle does not define you but what you do next does. Be defiant!
- Give yourself permission to fail and find the lesson you are to learn from it.

Living Life by Design

- Be determined. Everything happens for a reason. Self-reflect and figure out why. Find what will motivate you and use it as your drive to succeed.
- Be dedicated. Schedule an hour on your calendar twice a week and make it sacred. If you do not schedule it, you will keep saying, "I forgot to do it," thus delaying your comeback.
- Be disciplined. If life were easy, we would all be millionaires, right? There are no shortcuts. Overcome defeat and put in the work necessary to get it done!

Glenda Oakley Cook is a Transition Strategist, Leadership Coach and Market Place Mentor. Utilizing her experiences as an Army "Brat," former Army Captain and current Army spouse, she helps women take command of their lives to command the life they desire. A master at adapting and overcoming obstacles, breaking barriers and slaying societal statistics, she is quickly emerging as a millennial empowerment expert.

Glenda founded the Institute of Transitions, a consulting firm specializing in personal and professional development with an emphasis on transitions, leadership and confidence. Her firm's courses, training, events and coaching programs prepare emerging influencers with the ability to transition into their next stage of life with ease!

A combat veteran and a net worth over a half-million dollars by the age of 30, Glenda truly believes you can achieve anything with determination, dedication and discipline. She has been featured on over 40 different websites and publications; including the hit national television show on Esquire Network, *Friday Night Tykes*.

Most known for an innate ability to connect with her audience through dynamic and authentic speeches, she brings over 12 years of experience speaking to varying audiences. Having graced the same stages as Governors and Senators alike, she is ready to empower your audience! She is the founder of The Salute movement; honoring women for all that they balance in terms of life, family and career. Join her at SaluteSuccess.com. Her Philosophy—*"If you transition your mindset, you will transition your life!"*

SEVEN

Thriving Through a Season of Grief
BY GWEN WEBBER-McLEOD

Defining Resilience

Every woman has a significant story to tell, and many of you will relate to mine about the resilience I found by overcoming grief as a leader.

In my role as president and CEO of Gwen Inc., a private sector leadership development corporation, I spend a significant amount of time supporting women leaders. Thriving through grief is one of the most difficult aspects to discuss, partly because women are socialized to believe that regardless of our circumstances we must be strong for everyone but ourselves. The myth of the "Strong Woman" reigns. My leadership journey includes many moments of looking perfect on the outside, while being a complete "hot mess" on the inside. These moments make women feel as if we will not survive.

Knowing the myths about grief abound gives me courage to be transparent about my own experiences and how Gwen Inc. was launched during such a turbulent period. I hope my story inspires you to consider because grief cannot be avoided, you should develop life strategies enabling you to thrive, versus simply survive, through your most difficult moments. With that said, my beautiful sister, here is my story and I am sticking to it. My success as a woman leader is directly connected to the resilience I developed by breaking through after a breakdown during a season of grief.

Grief is often described as a never-ending time of darkness. I believed this too until life caused me to find resilience while facing ten nonstop years of grief. This experience taught me being resilient is the capacity to break through after multiple breakdowns.

My Story

I took great pride in being a serial entrepreneur since 1990, with each business venture leading to the incorporation of my legacy-building business, Gwen Inc. Five years into building my first business, my family experienced a life-altering experience.

"She has cancer."

We could hardly comprehend what our pediatrician had just said—our beautiful daughter had cancer and needed to be rushed to a regional hospital with a pediatric oncology unit.

Ashley was diagnosed with acute lymphocytic leukemia on December 22, 1995. She was only ten years old. It was startling to learn, as other children with similar symptoms were only said to have the flu. We were devastated. As my husband and I cried hysterically, we knew we needed to find a way to explain this to Ashley, and be the strong, loving and supportive parents we were. How could we tell her?

When we broke the news to her she took off running to her bedroom. With the help of an American Girl "Addie" doll we finally coaxed Ashley out of the bed and off to the hospital where she began five years of very aggressive leukemia treatment. It was a miracle in so many ways because 95 percent of her bone marrow as cancerous at diagnosis.

That was my first big encounter with grief. Although Ashley was in the hands of God and great doctors, the experience knocked me to the ground. It was the first time I recognized I had no control over anything. As a mother I had always been able to fix her life in twenty-four hours or less. But leukemia taught me that it was in control and in order for her to get well I had to surrender my daughter to God and her physicians and let them work to save her life.

Through the stress, I did some of the best work of my career. My partners and I built a successful marketing and project management business. I served on many powerful boards of directors and won several significant awards for being an outstanding woman leader in my state. I had breakthroughs during the day and broke down at night when worry set in: Would Ashley die? How could I be a good wife and mother to our five-year-old son who was devastated by his sister's illness? Could I continue being a successful entrepreneur? I spiraled into paralyzing despair.

Recognizing and Removing the Enemies of Resilience

I consulted a psychiatrist who asked me, "If I suggested you might be clinically depressed what would you say?"

I burst into tears and said, "Thank you, because I need to name this feeling." Then my lifelong secret flew out of my mouth. I had been feeling this way frequently throughout my life and had learned to survive and push through, but now I could not push any longer.

My doctor said to me, "Gwen, I am excited to help you through this time. I believe God has given you very special gifts and you need to get well to share them."

In the moment I decided I would thrive in the midst of the grief versus simply survive.

In the moment I decided I would thrive in the midst of the grief versus simply survive. I recognized sometimes we must break down to break through. I was treated for clinical depression throughout Ashley's treatment. Each session I felt stronger and stronger. I emerged healthy, incubating an idea for what would become my current company, Gwen Inc.

Although being an entrepreneur was quite fulfilling, I was made an offer I could not refuse and reentered the workforce. I left my business and became the director of communications at a nationally recognized women's college where the president was a close friend and colleague. She was about to make a bold leadership move and needed my help. As director I managed national media as the president transitioned the historic women's college into a coed institution. I also continued my entrepreneurial ventures by developing a small consulting practice that provided strategic planning and facilitation services. I was able to do all these things as I healed from a devastating moment in my life. I assumed my season of grief ended.

Then ...

We were at my parent's house on the eve of the new millennium, and my spirit was ready to celebrate after five long years of battling cancer. Our daughter was in remission and my father had just won a historic political campaign by being elected the first African American county legislator in his county. We were there to attend his swearing-in ceremony on New Year's Day.

During the evening my mother spoke to me while playing Solitaire on her computer. Without looking at me, she whispered, "I think your father might have cancer."

I said, "What?"

She repeated her suspicion and told me my father would see the doctor the following week.

The next day we proudly joined my father at the ceremony and it was truly one of the most beautiful days for our family. But my intuition was again working overtime; I knew something was very wrong. I had developed the "waiting for the other shoe to drop" syndrome and my anxiety kicked in again.

A few weeks later my father told us he had lung cancer with the prognosis of three to six months to live. How could this have been true? It was not fair! Ashley had just gone into remission! How would we fight cancer again knowing there would be no remission for my father? My husband, daughter and young son joined me in an extended season of grief, and we identified a talented family therapist who did grief work with us throughout the ordeal.

Of course my instinct was to put on the "Strong Woman" face and attempt to survive through it all. However, by then I learned it was possible to thrive in difficulty and opted to allow myself to break down knowing a breakthrough would come.

Turning Reactions into Resilience

While I continued working I asked God, "How is it even possible that You have me out here doing Your good works and You know I am completely crazed by grief?" Yet day after day, in the midst of another dark hour, I got up, got dressed, trusted God and carried on as an effective leader, good wife and mother.

I surrendered to the idea that I was being prepared for greatness and decided to press on, sadness and all.

What motivated this daily ritual was an inkling of an idea. In that season of grief another possibility emerged. What if learning to thrive through grief had something to do with preparation for greatness? Was it possible that developing the skill of breaking through after a breakdown was connected to giving me the capacity to lead at a very high level? Those tiny, but consistent thoughts changed my grief experience from one of constant sadness to a study in executive leadership. Deep, down inside I knew I would not be placed in those situations for no reason. I surrendered to the idea that I was being prepared for greatness and decided to press on, sadness and all. In the midst of my tears I reflected on leaders who came before me and what they endured to fully become who they were created to be. It was a good thing I did. Shortly after this epiphany I had to thrive through grief again.

My father died six months later, and as mourners came through to pay their respects, I stood in my grief proud to be his daughter, unbroken because I felt myself breaking through to greatness.

Throughout this tragedy, a college friend, Captain William (Billy) F. Burke, Jr., FDNY, was in touch with my family and me often, offering kindness and support. He was empathetic, as he too had lost his father and was still in a season of grief years later.

In 2001, on a beautiful September morning, Billy was called to work for what was thought to be a weird accident at the World Trade Center but was actually a horrifying terrorist attack. In an act of heroism my dear friend got all his men out of those towers and ran back in to help others. Shortly after he reentered the towers collapsed, killing him.

Grief again overwhelmed me and was now compounded because I never fully recovered from grieving the loss of my daughter's health and the death of my father. I was on my bathroom floor begging God to give me some relief. As always, God answered my requests, and He picked me up and sent me back into the world to do His will. I found myself screaming again at God, asking, "Why am I still standing? I should be broken into one million pieces!" But God would not let me fall apart; I still had a purpose to fulfill.

Billy's death made me realize there are no accidents in life. My trajectory to leadership in all its joy and challenge was carefully designed to position me for a significant leadership position. As I pieced together the events of my season of grief, the lessons learned taught me something specific about leadership.

I discovered leaders cannot control everything but can do their best to manage in difficulty. I learned to think critically on a daily basis, as each day had to be carefully designed to enable me to grieve and lead effectively at the same time. I understood the importance of self-care and allowed myself days to do nothing but engage in rest, self-reflection and rejuvenating activities.

Of utmost importance, I learned to live with intention because you never know when your time might come. I realized each of the lessons grief taught me were being used by the most effective leaders I knew. It became clearer to me that God used grief to help me find my purpose, which seemed to be helping leaders achieve personal and professional success.

Of utmost importance,
I learned to live with intention
because you never know
when your time might come.

During my work, I had noticed a pattern in emerging and established leaders who quietly floundered while attempting to achieve business goals. Leaders in organizations often arrived at their positions as a result of technical ability or longevity. I observed that a gap occurred when technical skills did not extend to the strategic relationship-building necessary to motivate, mobilize and inspire employees. I also witnessed that when leaders were not intentional about developing their own skills they experienced feelings of inadequacy and found themselves at a loss as to where to go for help.

The synthesis of attributes I developed during my season of grief—confidence, competence, courage and calm—became the traits I wanted to focus on with other leaders. I felt myself preparing to step out on faith to become a great leader and knew this: greatness was being birthed in me during grief, but there was still more work to do.

Within months of Billy's death, my best friend Joanne Reddick received a cancer diagnosis that took her life on September 5, 2003. After her funeral, my mother, two of my three sisters and I attended the Miss America Pageant. Although my grief accompanied me, I managed to have a good old, wild and wooly Webber-women time.

We engaged in our annual exchange of information giving specific instruction if one of us died and left our children alone. It seemed a meaningless exercise because the Webber girls had every intention of being sassy senior citizens on the dance floor.

Then the unthinkable occurred.

In December of 2003, my sister Terri and her daughter were in the midst of a happy moment when Terri said she could not breathe. Minutes later, my beautiful, vibrant, seemingly healthy sister died from sudden cardiac arrest in front of her daughter.

As devastating as my sister's death was, my previous experiences, combined with the leadership lessons, helped me thrive through this season of grief with greater ease.

The Power of Living Life by Design

My sister's death was the experience that had the most impact on my leadership. The entire time I was in this season of grief I distracted myself by fantasizing about a company that would help people become better leaders. For years this little thought became a place of solace and peace. Each year and each grief experience caused me to further develop this fantasy of a business from an idea into a full vision. I was fearful to ask God to help manifest it because what if I was not ready to be the company's formal leader?

The day eventually came when I was forced to speak life into my idea.

The day eventually came when I was forced to speak life into my idea. In 2004, as I was on the phone with my mother she asked how I was doing. I replied, "Mommy, I am either going to crawl to the bottom of my bed and never come out or I am going to do what I believe I have been called to do." I wanted to consciously pursue my purpose through this business.

She encouraged me to step out on faith and begin building the business. This meant leaving the comfort of my work at the time and stepping into the many unknowns that come with entrepreneurship. I was still hesitant and said I would think about it.

But God had other ideas ...

A former client called me to submit a project proposal, but I was dodging with claims that I felt too grief-stricken to do the work. In reality, I knew taking this position would catapult me into the creation of the business I had spoken about to my mother. I avoided the client for days but then, in a moment of flippancy, I asked, "How much are you going to pay someone to do this work?" The fee was the amount of my entire year's salary and I could earn that and more in six months. I hung up the phone and said, "Really God?" I prayed, took a breath, and resigned from my position that day.

I had no job, believing my family was destined to eat Ramen noodles indefinitely. Once again, God stepped in. Shortly after quitting my job, while I was walking the beach and talking to Him, I reflected on the ten-year season of grief and had a powerful thought. If I created the business, it had to be the place where I manifested my purpose, the one that became clear to me while I grieved the loss of my loved ones. The business would use the many lessons learned during my season of grief to help other leaders. I felt prepared and ready to lead the company. If I could endure it all during that season, there was no reason I would not be strong enough to create and lead the business I would call Gwen Inc.

Within three years of that walk on the beach I formally incorporated Gwen Inc. and now am the president and CEO. The company exists for the sole purpose of helping leaders achieve personal and business goals by focusing on the characteristics of confidence, competence, courage and calm. We serve emerging and established leaders across the country. Gwen Inc. is not only my business, it is my ministry, born from allowing leadership lessons to emerge through a season of grief.

I hope my story resonates with you. As women leaders it is important to experience all life has to offer including the leadership lessons you can learn during a season of grief. My eventual willingness to perceive grief as an opportunity to grow and develop into a strong woman leader helped me overcome factors that worked against my definition of resilience—the ability to break through after each breakdown triggered by grief. For me those factors were fear, depression and hesitance to become the woman God created me to be.

Making the conscious choice to intentionally thrive through grief, to believe I would be a better leader as a result of those experiences led to me mustering the courage to create and lead a business that is changing the lives of thousands of people each year. I offer the following to assist you as you grow and develop into a confident, competent, courageous and calm woman leader.

Pursue Resilience

- **Practice thriving versus surviving through grief.** It is easy to solely focus on being sad during a season of grief. However, as women leaders we must continue to lead at home and work. Pay specific attention to what you learn about yourself during grief. What specific actions did you take to get through day to day? What successes did you achieve while grieving? Document these experiences in a journal so they are available as a resource for future seasons of grief.

- **Leverage grief as a resource for greatness**. Great leaders have the capacity to endure pressure. The pressure of grief can be unbearable, or it can be leveraged to inspire greatness. Thriving through grief develops the attributes of patience, perseverance, strength and the ability to gain and sustain calm, all attributes found in strong women leaders.

- **Grief is not to be handled alone**. The myth of the "Strong Woman" hinders the grief experience. It also impedes your development as a leader. Successful women leaders have an inner circle of friends who serves as mentors, coaches and compassionate colleagues. Engage these women during periods of grief. Use them to help process important decisions. Invite them to review written documents, and seek their feedback regarding how you are leading while navigating the dynamics of grief. This support from your inner circle helps you maintain focus and effectiveness as a leader thriving through grief.

Living Life by Design

My story is written to encourage you to live life by design. Here is what I learned about this concept during my season of grief.

- **Consciously pursue your purpose**. Every woman has a calling or purpose. Use life experiences to help identify yours. My purpose became clear during a season of grief. Once I understood my purpose was to help emerging and established leaders, everything I did was with the intention of developing the philosophies, skills and behaviors required to act on my purpose through Gwen Inc.

- **Incubate and act on your wildest dreams—they will come true!** Fantasizing about Gwen Inc. began as a grief-management strategy. Just thinking about my business provided a mental vacation during a very difficult time. However, in time, the fantasy became a realistic option for me to pursue. The truth is Gwen Inc. manifested as a result of dedicated time to simply envisioning all it could be. When it was time to "birth" the company, I had already given so much thought to it that I created a business plan and incorporated the company in two years. Do not be afraid to incubate good ideas related to your wildest dreams and act on them when the time seems right. They will come true and allow you to live the life you were created to live, a life designed by you, for you.

Gwendolyn (Gwen) Webber-McLeod, M.S., is President/CEO of Gwen, Inc. She has over 30 years' experience in leadership development, facilitation, strategic planning and the development of effective coalitions/collaborations. Gwen is a frequently sought after lecturer and conference keynote speaker on the topic of leadership. Her clients are CEOs, executive and mid-level managers, and leadership teams in public, private, health care and education. Gwen is a cum laude graduate of SUNY Potsdam University, and a recipient of a Master of Science in Management from Keuka College where she graduated magna cum laude. Gwen takes pride in being a serial entrepreneur who created two businesses prior to Gwen, Inc.

In 2008, she incorporated her "legacy building" business, Gwen, Inc., which houses her consulting practice consisting of two new divisions: Gwen Inc.'s hallmark division—*The Leadership Connection®: A Resource Centered on Great Leadership*—opened as a resource center for leaders in January 2009. It is unique in that its sole resource is access to a team of talented leaders positioned to provide direct support to emerging and established frontrunners and leadership teams. And *"You Can't Fail Because Your History Says You Can't"*—a day celebrating professional women of color is the second division.

Gwen is the recipient of many awards, is affiliated with several organizations and writes a monthly column, *The Leadership Journey*, for Auburn's home town newspaper, *The Citizen*.

Connect with her at www.GwenInc.com.

EIGHT

The Press—
FIGHTING BACK BECAUSE YOU HAVE TO
BY KIM CHEATHAM

Defining Resilience

I'm not saying that I have this all together, that I have it made. But I am well on my way, reaching out for Christ, who has so wondrously reached out for me. Friends, don't get me wrong: By no means do I count myself an expert in all of this, but I've got my eye on the goal, where God is beckoning us onward—to Jesus. I'm off and running, and I'm not turning back. - Philippians 3:12-14, (MSG)

In 2000 I came to a crossroads. I could have either traveled the route of a mediocre lifestyle and easily accepted a handed-down career, or taken a detour toward the path to step up, take control and press. At that pivotal time I learned something profound about building resilience. It comes when you get tired of being tired. For me it required a change in direction, or a rerouting; a mental shift. I made a conscious choice to not allow anything or anyone stop me from reaching my fullest potential. When I programmed this attitude into my personal and professional GPS, it was then that I became successful. What I am saying is I turned into the person I knew was inside of me all along. Fear tried to consume me during those difficult times. I stuck to my conviction of something good would come out of it. It was for that reason I confessed every day, "Something good is going to happen to me today." The resilient leader I have become can now withstand the pressure that accompanies a battle with the will and expectancy to win—*the press*. I now can experience the greatness of my divine and precious oil. To this end, in remaining *faithful, pliable, and committed* I journeyed to resilience—mastering change and moving forward in spite of setbacks.

My Story

"There's no passion to be found playing small—settling for a life that is less than the one you are capable of living."[1] *– Nelson Mandela*

I barely made it through high school. We lived in Wisconsin where my parents worked outside the home to provide for their four children. I was the independent child. I would not ask for help even when I knew I needed it. My siblings and I were required to bring home good grades. However, the consequence of getting unsatisfactory marks was to get a whipping, be grounded or both. When report cards were distributed I already knew what to expect so I would prepare for the worst. I guess in a sense I had become somewhat impervious to the punishments since they did not change my hardheaded behavior. Being young and irresponsible, neither did I understand or recognize the impact it would have on my future. I soon learned how living only for the moment would be so costly.

Something within me cautioned I would not become a national statistic. I did graduate. Getting a good-paying job was what we were raised to expect after high school. But even then with bad grades and all, I wanted to climb the corporate ladder.

My work ethic made available many entry-level opportunities. But while steadily working hard, I noticed others in the company were getting promoted whereas I was passed over. I had all kinds of thoughts racing through my mind: "I am a high performer?" "When will it be my turn?" Still I would find myself humbly saying those supportive words, "Something good is going to happen to me today." In my mind, I believed not having a formal education smothered my chance for promotion. That epiphany was the missing piece to my personal development. Although I could not correct my past, I did develop an insatiable appetite to design my future. I have learned the art of resilience is not for the fainthearted, and neither is it selfish. By that time I was married with children and had to find a way to make an indelible footprint for them to follow.

Who would I be if I were to step out on faith and give voice to my heart?

Who would I be if I were to step out on faith and give voice to my heart? What could I become if I made the necessary adjustments to alter the landscape of my life? The time had come. If having a degree would swing open the doors to a better career and life, I was ready to walk through them—though I still believed hard work should pay off too.

I registered for classes at Concordia University. Because I did not do well in high school, the requirement was to obtain a grade of B or higher in basic math and English classes to be accepted in the associate degree program. Nothing would stop me now; I was empowered by the challenge. I arrived at Concordia even more obsessed with proving myself because the world was waiting for the value I could bring to them. And I did it with faith in myself and my God.

I did receive A's in those classes. That gave me the gumption to use everything within me to forego all signs of hopelessness. By then my confidence had soared. During that time I worked as an administrative assistant at Metavante Technologies. I completed the associate degree and transferred to another division of Concordia to pursue my bachelor's degree. The cost per credit hour was more reasonable and corresponded with the tuition reimbursement plan offered by my employer.

Midway to completing my bachelor's degree, the unthinkable happened. Metavante was acquired by FIS Global and afterward my entire department was downsized as part of a reduction in force. I was unemployed. Even if you have to go through a big trial, it helps to know you have what is needed to press your way over. That was undoubtedly one of those times for me. Still, together with confidence in my skills and experiences obtained on the job and in college, I saw that hard change as my next opportunity. Using the influence gained through my hard work, I believed I could successfully network.

...I saw that hard change as my next opportunity.

You should take advantage at every juncture for leaving where you are to get where you want to be. I desired so much more as a professional. My stubborn independence had held me captive for too many years. I can still remember those whippings because of it. I truly needed help and it was time to acknowledge it. When an idea leaps from your belly you must move into action.

After the company downsized, I learned my former manager had been hired by Johnson Controls where I also had an eye on a position that paralleled my skills and experience. Once I applied there, I reached out to her. She recommended me to the Human Resources department. I was interviewed and offered a position to support the CEO. During my interview with him, he asked where I saw myself in five years. I responded, "I want to be on your team but not as your assistant." I explained further I was 16 months from completing my bachelor's in business and wanted to be a business analyst working with sales and development. At that time he probably did not have much confidence in my business acumen. But I would not allow that nagging suggestion bring doubt to my dream or crush my self-confidence.

Recognizing and Removing the Enemies of Resilience

I knew for me to discover my purpose, fulfill my destiny and leave a legacy for my family, I needed to embrace some serious changes. I invested in myself and hired a life coach. I learned self-discipline and also trained my mind and will to become focused and pliable. And I relied on God's strength and wisdom. Returning to school as a wife and mother with a full time career, even with the support of my family, the true press began. It was a challenge and also a sacrifice for them. We nevertheless learned how to be flexible and respectful of each other. If I had a heavy workload or a class assignment due, we would sometimes have to eat out and the laundry was put on hold. But when those papers came back with A's on them, the entire family celebrated.

Having earned my bachelor's degree, I asked to meet with the CEO. People tell me I have a gentle, sweet spirit, however on that day, with a firm determination I said to him, "I am ready now for more of a challenge to begin building my career." I shared with him ideas and better ways the teams could report their monthly stats and how to improve their turnaround time with the sales team. He asked me to give him time to think about our conversation. Does the resilient one settle for what others think we should have? Of course not. Are we not the designers of our future? Yes we are. As Pastor Joel Osteen is quoted, "Once you know you're a 'no lack' person, you won't run away from that management position, thinking that you're not qualified, you'll run to it knowing that you're well equipped."[2]

Within two weeks a business analyst position was created for me. I began to work with the sales team as a business analyst and tradeshow manager plus enjoyed an increase in my salary. Had I not stepped up to voice my confidence in my value, this probably would not have happened. And afterward, the reality of 'something good is going to happen to me' kicked in again. Inside a year the team's dynamics changed. The CEO was moved to another area. By now I was familiar with accepting change as a setup for the next opportunity. With more responsibilities and another salary increase, I began an advanced business analyst position working with the program management team and engineers.

I made a quality decision to mindfully step out of victimhood and press into victorhood.

I made a quality decision to mindfully step out of victimhood and press into victorhood—empowering myself with divine guidance, faith and accepting change to get me there. To remain pliable I sacrificed attending social activities in my commitment to focus on my work and studies. Hard work does have its rewards. This time I walked into better opportunities. Promoted again, I was asked to join the client relationship management team as sales analyst where I enjoyed managing a team in Mexico, traveled abroad and having a private office.

The press is extremely necessary if you want to see the end of your objective. Persisting through it has produced many opportunities for me. I was placed in the midst of great leaders and drawn closer to where I wanted to go. Not only did they mentor me, but I was challenged to fight for my future. Since we know obstacles and setbacks—like standing, sitting and sleeping—are a part of life, persevering in spite of them is equally essential and is what kept me humbled and confident. I am a resilient woman who believes the best is still yet to come. And with the best, the worst will find a way to emerge. And it did.

Turning Reactions into Resilience

In 2012, at the height of my third promotion requiring a lot of travel, and in the midst of completing my bachelor's, I received a call from my father. He was not feeling well and had not been to see a doctor in a while. I realized this was a warning sign so when I returned from the business trip I went to check on him and to get him to the doctor. After some testing we were given the grueling diagnosis—prostate cancer.

No one is ever ready for the illness press. You have to face it head on. Standing firm and steadily focused during prior hardships had perfected my ability to brave this out with a loved one. Dad needed me. I was the only one there for him. My parents were divorced. My oldest sister had passed away from an asthma attack at the age of 28 and my other two siblings were busy with their own lives. I had to go through this press with him. Believing, encouraging, listening and caring when someone is in trouble is a true honor.

I had to go through the press with him.

With the report of having cancer, my father needed a few days to process the news. I was leaving on another business trip the following week. He did agree to further testing. However, there was a three-week wait for an appointment. There was no time to panic so I threw myself into networking mode and called my personal physician and explained the dilemma. He volunteered to contact his colleagues for help. We got an earlier appointment to "threat the cancer," putting it into remission for eight months. But during the ninth month the blood test count began to increase again. My father was obviously not feeling well and began to limp. The cancer had spread.

He was the toughest man I knew. My dad was so strong he would only take Tylenol to bear the pain. I needed some time to gather myself after learning about the sudden change in the hormone controller requiring him to succumb to chemotherapy twice a week. I was angry. My mind was infused with thoughts of a man who had retired three years prior after working for more than 20 years. No longer could he fish or hunt for recreation or travel to his home in Tennessee. Cancer. I was tired of hearing this word. I was devastated by seeing what it did to people. I was literally numb. As this ghastly malignancy spread to other parts of his body, I saw how chemo had taken out his hair. I also saw the child-like look in his eyes as I comforted him. How could this be happening? I needed my daddy. My children needed their grandfather.

My sister and daughter helped with taking him to his chemotherapy and doctor appointments. The support made a huge difference especially as anxiety peaked. Looking back over my life, I was the child my parents were concerned about—the strong willed, creative but independent youngster who did not fit into their mold. How did I work full time, travel on business, exercise my responsibilities as wife, mother and friend who served in ministry at my church find the time and tenacity to be a caregiver to my father?

I found a way to master the challenge—being proactive instead of reactive and remaining faithful in fighting alongside him. I was pliable when necessary and committed to do whatever it took to get through it as the victor.

When I received my graduation invitations I took one to my father. He looked at me and said, "Baby, I am so proud of you. I will not be there but your mom will." Devastated, I hung it on the wall next to his favorite chair. I did not want to hear him speak about his leaving this earth, but those conversations had become a part of our talks. Even though I loathe having these discussions with him, I knew I had to fight through my feelings and be responsible for his wishes. Know that you cannot make feelings go away, but you certainly can move through them.

Know that you cannot make feelings go away, but you certainly can move through them.

My father passed away two weeks prior to my graduation. On the eve of his death I was with him late into the night because he was not feeling well. As I sat next to him, he did not look like my daddy but more like a child. He awakened and told me to go home to take care of my family.

I called him several times the following morning but he did not answer. I could feel something was not right. I needed to leave work and go to check on him. I called my husband to meet me there.

We arrived the same time. As I put my key in the door I discovered the door was chained from the inside. I called out to him but there was no response. Looking at my husband, he knew what we had to do.

Thrusting his shoulder into the door, we pushed our way in. What we discovered was another 'unthinkable.' My father was in bed with his hands raised, eyes opened and feet cold as ice. I closed his eyes and cried. I had learned so much about him during the prior two years—his childhood, family and his life journey. Remembering how we sat together the night before talking and praying for each other, I was not ready for this press! I do not think anyone would be.

The day of my father's funeral, a letter confirming my bachelor's degree came in the mail. Family was here from out of town, so I shared my good news with them. In this press I knew a relentless person was emerging which gave me strength as I walked across that stage the following week. On the morning of my commencement ceremony, my husband—love this man—gave me a locket with my father's picture inside. The courage to stand when the pressure is on is gutsy resilience.

The courage to stand when the pressure is on is gutsy resilience.

The staff at Johnson Controls supported me throughout the journey with my father. At his funeral, the director of my team, an Air Force veteran told me this, "The way you took care of your father was truly honorable. You are a daughter of daughters." His words strengthened me. I knew the burden was lifting and I was never going to be the same. I was honored and thankful to be a caregiver to my father. I knew then I had to continue my education. I wanted to leave a legacy for my children and for their children as well.

The Power of Living Life by Design

When you stay firm and add power to whatever is intimidating you, it acts as a defense steering you to release your untapped potential. One of the viable byproducts in this process is the ability to remain humble and build confidence. You will also discover an unprecedented desire to disconnect from the past and embrace the future. And more importantly, in your growth you must continually invest your time, commitment and money in preparation for the ride.

Six months after my father passed away, I received my bachelor's in business from Concordia. During a meeting with the CEO at Johnson Controls, I noticed his master's degree certification hanging on his wall. While discussing it with him he told me to consider obtaining one as well. I boldly and proudly shared I was the first one in my family to obtain a bachelor's and one day I would like to teach the adult accelerated college courses. We both agreed. After that conversation and acknowledging what I felt in my gut to be my next season, I registered for classes at Concordia and my candidacy to the master's degree program was accepted.

My traveling increased at work so I was a few weeks overdue for my mammogram. I was elated I got a Saturday appointment because this was more convenient. During a routine mammogram one year to the date of my father's passing, I laid on the table for a biopsy of tissue that was not there the year before. I took a break from school. Somehow I felt I would not be alone in this. I knew God was with me. The tissue tested positive for breast cancer—stage 1 according to the size of the mass. Surgery was immediately scheduled. The doctors assured us it was very treatable and had been caught early. Because of the density of my breast, I would not have felt the lump, as it was far back in the tissue.

Ladies, your health must be a priority. Never hesitate to schedule your annual checkups. Because I faithfully attended to my health, the affected area was seen on the film. They were able to perform a comparison of the exam results from the prior year to determine the change in the tissue. For this I was thankful.

> Ladies, your health must be a priority.

Ten days after surgery I received a call from the surgeon. It appeared one of the margins of the mass was not clean and I needed a second surgery. While awaiting the results of this surgery I heard God speak to me, "No chemotherapy." Shaking and tearful I rushed to tell my husband. To my amazement he said, "I heard the same thing!" When you are faithful in the press there is no wiggle room for doubt and unbelief. So, accordingly my husband and I agreed I would not need chemotherapy. We said this each day.

There were four tests required. Test one results—no chemotherapy required to treat; Test two results—no chemotherapy; Test three results—no chemotherapy; Test 4—no chemotherapy. We stood in faith with what we heard our Creator say. I had not forgotten how chemotherapy affected my father. I did, however, agree to six weeks of radiation. The radioactivity caused noticeable and painful third-degree burns to my body so they had to stop the treatment. Shaken, humiliated and in pain, I sought counsel from my First Lady and Pastor the necessity of foregoing further treatments! How was this helping me?

I was committed to believing breast cancer was a lie. I cried, not because I was in fear, but more so because I did not have time for this—not now. I had finally gotten back in momentum with work and my studies. In addition, my new promotion was challenging but with many welcomed opportunities. And besides, no one in my family had ever experienced breast cancer. I will admit I was literally in shock—I was too young! Just when my strength was returning from the loss of my father, I had to relive seeing the same faces where my father was treated. I was determined and ready to fight for my life with everything within me. I had a long life planned for myself. I desired to see my children grow up. I wanted to experience being a grandmother, traveling the world with my husband and of course breaking through the glass ceiling in my career.

I realized if I was going to succeed in every area of my life, I had to give up worrying about what I perceived others thought about me. You have to love yourself enough to boldly go through the press with confidence. Resilience believes in oneself in the midst of circumstances, through every season and expects to grow from the challenge. It is the ability to turn one's life around and not look back. That was then and still is today a great chunk of my life plan.

You have to love yourself enough to boldly go through the press with confidence.

In the midst of the radiation treatments, I was scheduled to attend Dr. Deana Murphy's women's conference in Philadelphia. My husband agreed I should go and the doctor reluctantly released me to attend. The respite was exactly what I needed. When I boarded the plane that morning only two people knew of my condition. I was in so much pain! Still I met the most amazing women at that seminar.

I would slip out and go to my hotel room during the breaks to change my gel packs. I was definitely in the press for my life. I needed to be established mentally, physically and spiritually to complete the treatments when I returned home. Quieting my mind and meditating, a sense of refreshing came on me while I was there. My skin undoubtedly received the well-needed rest.

When I got home I was prepared to complete the remaining radiation treatments. Thank God I got through them successfully. For the next ten years I have to take a low dose chemotherapy pill every day. Pressing through the side effects of hot flashes and sporadic leg cramps, I still remain faithful and committed to the fact that I am healed. When your life is challenged, you quickly learn the true value of it and small things become so much more important. I press through for those I love, my husband who has always supported me and my children whom I want to see grow up and impact this world while building their own resilience.

When your life is challenged, you quickly learn the true value of it and small things become so much more important.

I have been faithful to and for so many others and now I needed the care and compassion that I so freely gave. I did not want to be the topic of discussion around my community as was my father. To avoid this, my husband and I agreed to be selective with whom we would share our problems. Hence, living life by design while in the press involved a commitment and the execution of some tough decisions. The wisdom gained in it, especially concerning relationships, created a positive lifestyle. I learned so much about the importance of spending quality time with those I love. Never allow the cares of this world take you away from pursuing your wildest dreams and desires. They are priceless.

Along with my undying faith and the support and love of my husband, Jumaane, my children, Suncierra, Cheyenne, Faith, and Joseph, my resilience has shined through the press. Now that my mind is transformed, I can use self-control. I have earned degrees and promotions and won victory over cancer. I am now two years cancer free. My life is a complete 180-degree turn from the girl who barely finished high school.

I am writing this chapter at three classes to completing my master's in marketing and holding a 3.8 grade point average. My family is blessed and my career is flourishing. Life and all it has to offer is precious. I am an opportunist. I am not afraid of the press nor of being resilient in the midst of it. The healing I received was a gift. There is so much more I still have to do—helping other women rise to their fullest potential, to press through all obstacles and to accomplish their heart's desire.

Because I learned to be *faithful, pliable* and *committed*, I am possible and so are you.

I leave you with what I know for sure:

Pursue Resilience

You must fight for yourself through resilience and never hide from it. In doing so, know this:

- The press is necessary. It discovers, develops and releases leaders.

- See the press as an occasion to become your best.
- Embrace change. Behind its door is a new opportunity.
- Invest in yourself. Have confidence in you because you are enough.

Living Life by Design

A life by design plans ahead the destination and fights its way through every obstacle to get there. You can do it if you:

- Believe that you are possible.
- Be pliable and willing to change for the better.
- Know this: “Something good is going to happen to you today.”
- Make yourself a priority.

Works Cited

[1]**Forbes. (2013).** http://www.forbes.com/sites/mfonobongnsehe /2013/12/06/20-inspirational-quotes-from-nelson-mandela

[2]**Forbes. (2012). http://www.forbes.com/sites/carminegallo/2012** /01/09/joel-osteen-7-keys-to-successful-public-speaking/

Kim Cheatham's professional voyage began more than 15 years ago when she discovered she loved bringing people together to improve customer and employee engagement. By the time she left her position as Business Analyst at Johnson Controls, she had significantly improved sales operations and executives from across divisions and geographies were enjoying the enthusiastic energy and encouraging results they were seeing. Kim took these skills into Sales Management guiding leaders in an ever-changing mission for effective approaches to customer relations management and training. She has trained sales teams in North America, Mexico, and Germany.

In her belief of paying-it-forward, she is currently a youth leader in her church community. Kim also serves as the Marketing Director for MKE Peace, a non-profit organization promoting peace through MKE peace rallies, networking events and bringing awareness to the community. Because of her passion to guide youth girls to live above mediocrity, she believes the same principles that produce performance success in the business world also applies to the personal performance in youth.

Kim is a leader who can withstand the pressure that comes with setting high expectations for herself, her family and her vocation. She is a two-year breast cancer survivor with an unwavering will and enthusiastic expectation to win.

A wife to Jumanne and mother to Suncierra, Cheyenne, Faith and Joseph, Kim earned a Bachelor of Business Administration from Concordia University where she will complete her master's degree in marketing in 2015.

Contact Kim at kmcheatham@wi.rr.com.

NINE

BEND BUT DON'T BREAK
BY MABEL JONES-HANSFORD

Defining Resilience

Let us take a moment and talk about resilience. What is it? What does it look like? Why do I need it? Is it important? Fundamentally, Webster defines resilience as "the ability to become strong, healthy or successful again after something bad happens; the ability of something to return to its original shape after it has been pulled, stretched, pressed, bent, etc."[1] My resilience is my ability to bend and not break. It is me bending whenever I needed to bend and, honestly, not bending when I probably should have. Resilience means gracefully coping when actually feeling inside like I am going to explode and crumble into little pieces. Thankfully, I hold on and recognize the strength in my personal power and all of the influences in my life. Thank you Jesus! Real talk, these are the things that have kept me from breaking. Resilience and the courage to be vulnerable are what characterize me as a phenomenal woman and leader.

My Story

As I open the door, welcome you in and share a few snapshots of my life, the first role of my journey was as a daughter. That little girl who lies deep down inside all of us women influenced and manifested itself in all my other roles as I matured into womanhood, navigating my existence through the maze called life. It was also the influence of all the other "isms" from the folks who gave me life and raised me that created and defined my strength, character, staying power and ability to rise up and be resilient, no matter what came my way.

Although it is certainly not a fairytale, my story begins as a tale like so many others. As a young black child raised in the '60s, it was definitely a time of turmoil. I was reared by parents who themselves struggled through this world. Their greatest grind was doing all they could with the little they had. They shielded their children from this awful time of unbelievable difficulty every day.

When I think about the sweet essence of resilience, the first vision that comes to mind is my mother angel, Mary Victoria Jones. She is a woman of great quiet strength and an amazing role model!

Mom, along with her nine siblings, experienced a very harsh and humbled childhood while growing up poor in rural Powhatan, Va. However, she got her high school diploma despite the substantial hardships against her. Similar to most families in the south during the '50s, mom followed her older siblings to the northeast for opportunities that were not available back home and simply for a better quality of life. Mom never attended college. She got a job working on an assembly line at Dumont Television Network. Mom was a very hard worker and a dedicated employee. She was committed to doing a great job. That opportunity provided steady income, employment and improved the quality of her life.

Mom and dad met in Paterson, N.J. They got married in 1959 and were blessed with a daughter and three sons. Although they worked hard to provide and take care of us, frankly, dad's alcoholism made life hellacious, unpredictable and fearful. Sadly, as long as I can remember, dad was a very unhappy, miserable and cold individual. Basically, he was not there for himself, nor was he able to be there for his family.

My introduction to the necessity of being resilient began by being raised in a dysfunctional home environment primarily due to an alcoholic father. As a child, I was consumed with feelings of anger, anxiety, shame and depression because of my dad's behavior when he was drunk inside and outside the home. I prayed and wished with all my heart that dad would be like the lovable and attentive fathers I saw on television. I wanted him to be a wonderful husband to my mom and a competent father to my brothers and me. Unfortunately, that was just another dream deferred.

Dad did not acknowledge, accept, nor seek help for his alcoholic disease. As a little girl, I certainly could not understand my father was actually suffering from a disease. I was so frustrated because I thought he was being stubborn and it was in his total control to stop drinking alcohol if he really wanted to. I was filled with rage and resentment because I believed dad chose alcohol over his family. Our feelings and needs were not a priority. Due to my father's alcoholism, my family suffered on so many levels—mentally, emotionally, spiritually and financially. On the outside, we appeared to be an example of a good ole black family with a mom and dad in the home. On the inside though, my mom was basically a single parent due to my father's lack of responsibility, dependability and willingness to be present.

Without complaining, mom picked up the slack and shouldered most of dad's duties as well as her own. Instead of focusing on the dysfunctional family environment that existed in our home, mom was dedicated and committed to loving, encouraging and raising her four children to the best of her ability. My brothers and I knew we could always depend on mom and she had our backs (sometimes literally).

Rather than allowing my father's alcoholism to break me, I made the decision to focus on my mom as my example of a positive, strong and inspiring role model. Mom was my shero! I became very driven, focused and goal oriented. For example, although I had no clue where the money would come from, I was determined to go to college, graduate and have a successful career in the business industry. To make that happen, I had to believe in myself, be confident and resourceful. I shared my aspirations with people of influence—guidance counselors, teachers, etc. They were very reassuring and provided me a wealth of information regarding financial aid and great business colleges and universities.

During the spring of 1978, I was accepted to Fairleigh Dickinson University, the largest private university in New Jersey, and majored in marketing. Four years later, with a Bachelor of Science degree, I was the first member of my family to graduate from college. Without being confident, purposeful, dedicated, conscious and willing to go above and beyond, that accomplishment would have never happened.

Without being confident, purposeful, dedicated, conscious and willing to go above and beyond, that accomplishment would have never happened.

From day one as a new college grad entering the financial

services industry, my plan was to demonstrate my value and skills by being an excellent performer and contributor. In addition, I wanted to learn as much as I possibly could. Unfortunately, that approach was not successful and did not protect me from being devastated after I got fired from my first significant job fresh out of college.

To provide you some background, I accepted a position as a manufacture representative with a major financial company that I was totally in awe of. My basic responsibilities were to service my book of business by ensuring my clients were aware of products and services that met their needs, sell those items and train the clients' staff on their use. In addition, I was responsible for business development. The company offered on-the-job training and a chance to travel across the United States. I was so overwhelmed that when I got hired I neglected paying attention to details and focusing on the fundamental job expectations.

The training was very substandard, but due to my intimidation, immaturity and silly pride, I ignored taking care of myself by speaking up and asking for additional help from the training team. I thought I would be viewed as stupid, weak and incompetent. Those thoughts and feelings also reminded me of my father's ugly, negative, derogatory remarks that haunted me and made me feel inferior time and time again.

In short, I did not perform the job I was hired to do. Once again, those old familiar feelings of anxiety, anger, embarrassment and depression resurfaced. Due to my inability to speak up and voice my need for more training, I understood I would eventually be placed on probation and ultimately fired if I did not improve. I was completely in denial, stuck and neglected to take action.

I will never forget the day my manager called me in her office and informed me I was being terminated. In the moment my ego was crushed. I felt like an eternal loser. Once I got over the shock of that failure, calmed down and accepted responsibility for the role I played in the situation, I recognized the lessons and blessings I gained. Failure was the best feedback I had received. Ironically, in the spirit of professional development, that experience laid a solid foundation and served as a teachable moment. It was also a catalyst for all future personal and professional adversities and victories.

Failure was the best feedback I had received.

Not realizing or admitting it at the time, getting fired from that job was actually a fortunate turning point in my life. I did not keep my eyes on the prize and I lost sight of the priorities of completely understanding basic job responsibilities and the role of success. Although that experience was indeed very traumatic, I was humbled and grateful for the wisdom I gained during the starting point of my career. Going forward in my profession, I did everything in my power not to ever repeat those same mistakes.

As I reflect over my positions, I have been the recipient of substantial adversities, failures and successes. My ability to bend and not break was primarily due to being blessed with great family, friends, awesome mentors and colleagues to lean on for guidance, support and inspiration during dark and rocky periods.

As an illustration, I relocated to Charlotte, N.C., in 1999 for family reasons, leaving a progressive career at Fidelity Investments in Irving, Texas, a city near Dallas. I joined The Vanguard Group as a team leader. Presenting a motivation for success, the management, fellow colleagues and staff welcomed me with open arms.

Remembering my prior painful termination experience, I paid attention to the job specifics and was totally engaged. I pursued opportunities to stretch myself to go above and beyond my new job requirements. I consistently demonstrated strong performance and leadership and advanced in various managerial roles.

However, relocating from the Dallas area to Charlotte was not as easy as I had anticipated. I carried the burden of my two sons, my mom and husband, who was unemployed seeking a job. Unbeknownst to me, my cup overflowed! Moreover, I desperately missed my support system of family, friends and old colleagues. Although I was overwhelmed and terribly homesick, I decided to change my perception of the situation and put an end to the ongoing pity party I celebrated on a daily basis. It was self-defeating and counterproductive. I gradually adjusted my attitude and focused on all of the blessings taking place in my life.

I completely embraced and envisioned the sky as the limit for my family and me in the new place we called home.

Essentially, my move provided a fantastic career opportunity with a major financial organization, full relocation package, good salary, bonus and the opportunity to live and raise my children in a beautiful and thriving city. Simply changing my attitude and perception of the situation, going with the flow, bending and not breaking down had a tremendous positive impact on the altitude of my career. I completely embraced and envisioned the sky as the limit for my family and me in the new place we called home.

During 2002, I again embraced change and accepted an opportunity to join Wells Fargo as a vice president and bank plan manager. I was extremely thrilled for this new role. My professional development and career would advance by joining a wonderful organization with occasion to serve a terrific leadership team, great colleagues and staff. From day one, without any hesitation, I became laser focused, excelled at performing my job and made contributions.

I would be remiss if I did not express my frustration and disappointment with the lack of diversity amongst the ranks of senior leadership. Not too many folks who looked like me held senior leadership positions. I refused to allow it to discourage or limit me. Rather than complain, I chose to get involved by joining an employee resource network and participating in numerous diversity trainings. My goal was to be a light of positive influence and pursue opportunities to take part in the solutions and not the problems.

I encouraged myself and tightly held on to my personal vision, dreams and intentions to thrive and serve as a change agent. My objective was to be an outstanding role model who led by example, motivated and inspired others to be confident, stay strong and focused, lean on their faith and never give up on themselves or their dreams and goals. Using that approach, I received back so much more than I could have ever imagined. I was able to develop, deepen and maintain valuable relationships with members of my corporate family and clients. I gained priceless transferable skills and competencies, such as an enthusiastic and open-door management style, visionary leadership, motivational speaking and excellent team building.

In terms of successful partnerships and friendships associated with numerous roles I have maintained in my life, the absolute most common denominator amongst all of them is my unapologetic spirit of resilience. Most would agree that relationships can be so precious, beautiful, fragile, good, bad, blessings and in some respects non-blessings. Over the years, these significant roles and relationships have stretched, tugged, humbled and bent me, but they did not break me. Through trial and error, I have crawled, walked, run and soared in each of them.

For example, being married to the love of my life and best friend for over 27 years has provided me an abundant amount of profound love, joy, peace and a sense of security. It has also challenged and required me to be strongly committed to the marriage and work very diligently through communication issues, problems, pain, frustration, disappointments, misunderstandings, obstacles and responsibilities. In my opinion, there is no such thing as a perfect marriage. You are going to experience highs and lows. Simply put, it is a reality of life. However, my marriage has certainly been a blessed union that has brought forth two amazing sons—Sean and Andre Hansford. As their parents, we are truly grateful for how much they have enriched, enlightened, elevated and transformed our lives. In addition to marriage, parenting is certainly no easy feat! Regardless of the roller coasters of life, my husband and I remain united to forge ahead, rise up and overcome the challenges of life.

Shortly after I gave birth to my sons in 1989 and 1993, I began to gradually pile on the pounds. I complained about the weight gain to whoever would listen, including myself, for days, weeks, months and eventually years. I would look in the mirror and not recognize the total stranger staring back at me. Rather than honestly acknowledging the root causes of my issues, owning them and making a strategic effort to change them, I cowardly blamed the weight gain on having children, work, menopause, aging, stress and whatever situation I could conveniently wrap my brain around and latch on to.

Once I became sick and tired of being sick and tired, I made a decision to pull myself up by my bootstraps and consistently work a practical plan that involved healthy foods, less cocktails, more water, exercise, a sufficient amount of sleep and meditation. I pursued a lifestyle that entailed mental, physical, emotional and spiritual balance.

To my surprise, I kicked it up a notch by accepting an invitation to join The Purple Butterflies, a wonderful female running club. On behalf of my health, that was definitely one of the best decisions I made. Furthermore, I had the most awesome time making new friends, fellowshipping with some of the most dynamic women who motivated and inspired each other and participating in 5K, 10K and half-marathon races. They were a group of amazing sisters who enriched my life on so many levels. It was a rocky start during practice sessions for each of us. However, running through the finish line and celebrating our races and marathon victories together was truly special because we never gave up.

I pursued a lifestyle that entailed mental, physical, emotional and spiritual balance.

Consequently, in regard to fitness, that was a life-changing experience for me. I accomplished my goals, gained a renewed sense of confidence and embraced my new, dear friend in the mirror. I was grateful for my decision to step out of my comfort zone, pursue that goal, remain committed and successfully hit those targets. Bull's-eye! Oh, what a wonderful feeling.

Recognizing and Removing the Enemies of Resilience

In my case, the enemies of resilience actually started with me. They were the negative chatter I created in my own mind and allowed to torture my spirit. You know those voices that echo in your head from the folks who said you could not, you should not and who do you think you are? The lack of confidence, feelings of inadequacy, fear and weakness began with negative childhood experiences of being raised in a dysfunctional family environment and with an alcoholic parent who never displayed love or interest in my mom, brothers or me.

Because of my father's alcoholism, his behavior and the way he treated his family, I felt unworthy, ashamed, unloved, less than and like I did not matter. I battled those internal demons and lies throughout my personal and professional life. I sabotaged myself by feeding into analysis paralysis and creating a deep-rooted fear that immobilized me from achieving my perfectly designed destiny as a child of God. I knew deep down in my soul there was something terribly wrong with my feelings, thoughts and how I viewed myself.

During those difficult and dark moments, I believed in my heart there was so much more to who I was.

During those difficult and dark moments, I believed in my heart there was so much more to who I was. I found the courage to demonstrate strength by being brutally honest and vulnerable enough to recognize I needed help to get through my fears, anxiety, panic attacks and depression. I courageously took an honest self-inventory, made some evaluations, paid attention to my environment, stood up and removed the people, places and things that served as toxic enemies.

I learned not to concern myself with hurting folks' feelings. I realized it was the very same concern that kept me stuck in a barrel of crabs and prevented me from moving to the top and onward to my divine destiny. That mentality can be disguised as guilt, shame, a false sense of responsibility and loyalty. Through trial and error I learned I possess the power and capacity to align my prayers, positive creative visions, great strategies, excellent teamwork and great processes with intentions and actions that produce exceptional results. As a case in point, the professional corporate success I experienced as a leader at The Vanguard Group and Wells Fargo was primarily due to those attributes.

Through hard work, doing the right thing, getting professional help and routinely taking a self-inventory of my strengths and weaknesses, I was determined to overcome my fears, work outside the box and follow the spirit that guides me. You all know and are able to recognize that feeling when you genuinely sense something so profoundly that it envelops your soul. That feeling is your spiritual guide. Surrender and go with it. It is also the presence of your resilience.

Turning Reactions into Resilience

Being informed, educated and aware of the characteristics of adult children of alcoholics has truly empowered me in many aspects of my personal and professional life. I can now relate to the following sample of characteristics that have negatively impacted my life:

1. Adult children of alcoholics judge themselves without mercy.
2. Adult children of alcoholics have difficulty having fun.
3. Adult children of alcoholics take themselves very seriously.
4. Adult children of alcoholics have difficulty with intimate relationships.
5. Adult children of alcoholics overreact to changes over which they have no control.
6. Adult children of alcoholics usually feel that they are different from other people.
7. Adult children of alcoholics are extremely loyal, even in the face of evidence that the loyalty is undeserved.[2]

Because of the knowledge I currently possess, I am mindful of those types of thoughts and behaviors and proactively counter them with positive thoughts and actions that enable me to live a healthy, happy, balanced and successful life. As I progressed through my professional career, when I encountered challenging situations, the warrior in me would fight back by countering my destructive thoughts with statements such as "I can do all things through Christ who strengthens me" (Philippians 4:13, *NKJV*); "I do matter"; "I am capable of making a positive difference"; "I am not inferior to anyone"; "I am not a victim"; and "I am victorious!" When I was feeling helpless and hopeless, I got down on my knees, prayed fervently and reached out to my close support network. When I was sad, I refocused my vision and thoughts to the things that made me smile, encouraged and inspired me. When I thought I could not go on, I pressed on anyway because I recognized it was not all about me. On countless occasions I was forced to bend, but I also bravely stood up and refused to break.

I know within my heart I am divinely created and being transformed for better.

Developing and strengthening my resilience muscle was not easy and it was definitely a gradual process that took shape one life incident at a time. I could not purchase or borrow it. My resilience propelled me to feed my soul when I had that burning desire in my belly of a dream or aspiration I was determined to accomplish. I believed in myself, maintained my faith and trusted the core of my inner strength.

I am a conqueror. I know within my heart I am divinely created and being transformed for better. My mindset, vocabulary, intentions, actions and capacity for continuing without weakening are the tools that build my creative spirit, nurture my genius and provide me with courage to persevere no matter what comes my way. Hallelujah!

The Power of Living Life by Design

It is critically important to know yourself, have the courage to "do you" and create a vision for your life regardless of the circumstances you are born into and experience. Without my own vision, my life would have been complicated and confusing because the design would have likely not been created by me, but by others. It would have been patterned by the people who raised me and the negative influences of my environment. In the beginning, I did not have direct control over any of it. From the time I was born, my parents had ideas about how they were going to raise me, how they would guide me and what they wanted my life to be. Please do not take this out of context; it is not always a bad approach. Most parents, including my own, had good intentions and wanted the very best for their children. They wanted their children's lives to be better than theirs.

Let us take a look at the famous Williams sisters, Venus and Serena. Regardless of their humble beginnings and the environment they grew up in, their father was determined to develop and guide them to tennis greatness. On the flip side of that are the parents who pushed their son or daughter to go to medical school when the child had absolutely no desire or interest in attending.

Oftentimes, after much struggle and uncertainty, we begin to realize something is wrong. We continue to struggle, believing this is what we have to do, but the real truth is we do not have to be or follow anything other than our own individual truth.

In spite of my difficult childhood, I was extremely ambitious, determined to live a joyful life full of success. I also wanted my family to be proud of me. Because my dad was an alcoholic did not mean I had to become one and live a sad and unhappy life. So I made a commitment to myself to dream big, set my goals high, work hard and soar.

Because my dad was an alcoholic did not mean I had to become one and live a sad and unhappy life.

Generational patterns continued to haunt me because I did the same things over and over again expecting a different result. Could that be insanity? Most often the patterns were unconscious. Like the interior designer who has a creation in mind, what if I took the time and carefully sketched out all the things I truly wanted and continued to make unique and valuable customized design changes as necessary? If I was brutally honest with myself, I might discover the initial design had flaws. Sometimes life shouts that you need to change or readjust the plan.

The best design to live life by is the one you truly desire, create and own for yourself. However, be flexible and open enough to know when it is not working and when changes are in demand. Also recognize when it is time to pause and consider "what if?"

Pursue Resilience

- Accept your truth. Do not hesitate to be true to yourself. You were divinely created for God's purpose. Embrace your unique creation and commitment.

- Acknowledge your fears. You cannot change what you do not acknowledge. Get to the root cause of your fears and address them directly.

- Embrace your passions. Trust your instincts. Believe in yourself and have faith in the desires of your heart. Be confident as you pursue your dreams and aspirations.

- Do not be afraid to hear "no." Typically, no just means not now. Never give up! Be persistent and follow up with all potential opportunities to learn and grow.

- Stand your ground. Demonstrate belief in yourself, your products and services. Reveal your morals and ethics as it relates to your profession, business or organization.

Living Life by Design

Please be advised by opening my door, welcoming you inside and sharing snapshots of my life's journey, my intention is to energize and empower you to embrace your life and live it by your unique design. Consider the following wisdom I gained:

- Accept yourself without any doubt or concern. Know you are special, valuable and that you matter to the universe. That is exactly why you still continue to exist.

- Know you are blessed and highly favored and created for God's unique purpose.

- Embrace who you are because everyone else's identity is taken or already assigned.
- As significant as your very own fingerprint, be true to yourself and do not hesitate to "do you" exceptionally well and unapologetically

In closing, I would like to leave you with my favorite quote by Theodore Roosevelt:

> The Man in the Arena
>
> "It is not the critic who counts; not the man who points out how the strong man stumbles, or where the doer of deeds could have done them better. The credit belongs to the man who is actually in the arena, whose face is marred by dust and sweat and blood; who strives valiantly; who errs, who comes short again and again, because there is no effort without error and shortcoming; but who does actually strive to do the deeds; who knows great enthusiasms, the great devotions; no spends himself in a worthy cause; who at the best knows in the end the triumph of high achievement, and who at the worst, if he fails, at least fails while daring greatly, so that his place shall never be with those cold and timid souls who neither know victory nor defeat."[3]

Works Cited

[1]**Resilience. (2015). Merriam-Webster.com.** Source: http://www.merriam-webster.com/dictionary/resilience

[2]**Addiction in Family. (2015).** Characteristics of ACOA by Janet G. Woititz. Source: http://addictioninfamily.com/alcohol/characteristics-of-acoa-by-janet-g-woititz

[3]**Almanac of Theodore Roosevelt. (2015).** Source: http://www.theodore-roosevelt.com/trsorbonnespeech.html

Mabel (MJ) Jones-Hansford, is a certified career transformational coach, author, motivational speaker and entrepreneur who provides clients with educational tools to make their careers and lives thrive by teaching how to be an agent of change. She provides professional developme nt training and laser focused customized coaching.

An 18 year former financial services business executive with strong knowledge of institutional retirement and trust, MJ served her diverse expertise in streamlining and managing operations and developing high performance teams while improving overall staff morale and quality client service. A strategic and multidisciplinary head in a gamut of Fortune 500 companies such as Fidelity Investments, The Vanguard Group and Wells Fargo (formerly Wachovia), MJ developed a reputation for being a competitive, enthusiastic visionary leader.

Having received the Wachovia Capital Management Group (CMG) Leadership Award and Wachovia's Retirement Services Team Excellence Award, MJ has combined her skills and competencies with her dynamic personality to deliver potent and creative experiences for her clients through excellent management, leadership and consulting.

MJ earned a bachelor's of science degree in marketing from Fairleigh Dickinson University. She currently resides in North Carolina with her family.

Reach out to her at MabelHansford@gmail.com.

TEN

BURDENS AND BLESSINGS
BY MELLANIE KAI LASSITER

Defining Resilience

Bruised but not broken.
Disappointed but not discarded.
Wounded but not weary.
Faint but not fearful.
Deceived but not desecrated.
Saddened but not jaded.
Left but not lonely.
I sometimes stumble and often fail but I always succeed.
I am resilient.

My Story

I have often said being a preacher's kid (PK), especially the daughter of a pastor, is both a blessing and a curse. Church folk have brought out the best and worst in me over the years. Although it would be easy for me to dwell on the negative, I have been much more impacted by the blessings of this journey.

PK life is all my siblings and I have ever known. My dad accepted his call to ministry in college and was already pastoring two churches by the time he graduated. Therefore, the title of first lady is all my mom has ever known too. Our family life was full of church services, revivals, auxiliary meetings, Bible studies, annual days and appreciation events. In between ministry activity, we enjoyed daily dinner together, Friday night outings, Sunday dinner and family vacations. We also lived through many midnight phone calls, funerals and burials, disagreements and deception, hospital visits and overall suffering. My family has seen it all.

As a PK, many expectations were placed on me and my siblings, both good and bad. On one hand, people say preachers' kids are the worst. Folks expect us to be mischievous and always up to something bad. On the other hand, preachers' kids are expected to be model children, always demonstrating perfection in our actions. Luckily for me and my siblings, my mom was a consummate advocate for her children. She always protected and defended us while encouraging us to just be ourselves. My dad is a second generation preacher who truly understands the perils of being a preacher's kid and constantly sought balance in our upbringing.

As a preacher and pastor, I guess my dad is ultimately responsible for all the burdens I have carried throughout life as his child. As a helpmate and first lady, my mom is equally responsible for birthing me into this situation. From each of them, I have learned many lessons on living and have experienced all the things I initially thought were burdens turn into infinite blessings.

I learned how to treat people from listening to my dad preach on Sunday mornings. But I learned specifically how a man should treat a woman and his family from observing dad every day. While other kids stopped at the corner store on their walks to school each morning, I enjoyed a hot breakfast cooked by him. My classmates had Corn Flakes and Sugar Smacks while my family enjoyed French toast, eggs, bacon, grits and sausage. Each day, dad packed our lunch boxes, often mixing up who ate the mustard versus who ate the mayonnaise, but we all had healthy meals for lunch. After breakfast, he walked us to the bus stop and debated the Bible with our Jehovah's Witness neighbors while we waited for the bus to arrive.

At the end of each school day, despite what was going on in the world, we sat down as a family to eat together and watch Lisa Thomas Laury anchor the local evening news. While we ate, dad asked us what we learned that day, scolded us for misbehaving and encouraged us to do our best. I remember when the Philadelphia 76ers won the NBA championship. I was in the fourth grade. My dad picked us up from school early and took us to the parade! He even tried taking us to the Thanksgiving Day Parade one year but we cried to go back home, as we were freezing in the bitter cold with no extra blankets or food. We were not at all prepared for the weather, but we enjoyed the opportunity to spend time with our dad. When we became teenagers, dad even drove us to parties with our friends on Friday nights, although all of our friends swore he would never let us out of the house. Little did our friends know—my dad was super cool!

Over the years, I was privileged to receive many accolades and dad never let the distance prevent his presence. He was there whenever I called him. He never missed a graduation and he was even present for the birth of both of his grandchildren. He prayed for us and with us. He even let us stumble and fall sometimes, always there when we got back up to dust us off and send us away again. I will never forget the time I was assaulted in college. Like a superhero, dad was on the first flight to be there.

Recognizing and Removing the Enemies of Resilience

Like most freshman students at Spelman College, I entered having graduated in the top tenth of my high school class and I thought I would easily excel in college just as I did in high school. Like most of my classmates, I also grew up in a family that stressed the importance of education and established high expectations for me. Not only was I expected to bring home good grades, I was expected to meet nice people and begin friendships that would ultimately last a lifetime.

While I accomplished the latter, I had a rocky start in the grades department. Instead of achieving academic success as a college freshman, I spent most of my time homesick from being so far away from my parents and the love of my life, my high school boyfriend. I returned from Christmas break on academic probation topped with threats from my parents of returning home for poor grades. On top of all that, little did my parents know, I was caught participating in underage drinking at a nearby campus and faced suspension, ultimately defending myself to a peer review council. As if that was not enough, at the end of second semester, my high school sweetheart revealed he was gay. I was devastated.

My family had no clue the number of issues I faced when I returned home after freshman year. When I finally got myself together during sophomore year, I was attacked one night and spent the remainder of the semester fighting nightmares and encouraging myself daily. I once again suffered in silence although I was constantly surrounded by family and friends.

Junior year of college marked a new start for me. I again begged my parents for one more opportunity to get it right and returned to school determined to make the best of it. And that I did. At the beginning of the school year, I found out the aunt of a good girlfriend had recently been placed in charge of the counseling center on campus. "Aunt Nancy," as we affectionately called her, summoned me to her office one day after hearing about my sophomore year experiences, realizing I was the girl she knew from her niece but had no idea I was the same girl who had been attacked the prior semester.

Sharing helped to heal my hurt and allowed others to help me with resources.

Aunt Nancy introduced me to "couch time," better known as therapy and it was the best decision I made that year. My therapy sessions were my first lesson on the power of sharing. Week after week I shared my fears, frustrations and failures with someone. Sharing helped to heal my hurt and allowed others to help me with resources.

Turning Reactions into Resilience

Growing up in church as the pastor's kid, my earliest lesson on leadership is now called the 11th commandment by my siblings and me: "Be ye always ready" (ref. Matthew 24:44, *KJV*). I never knew when I would be called upon to sing a song, read a scripture or say a prayer. Because of those experiences, I now know success comes when preparation meets opportunity.

From observing my mother in church, I learned the importance of women leaders. My mother taught me about Esther, a woman who was thrust into a leadership position within a male-dominated environment "for such a time as this" to be more than just another face in the crowd (ref. Esther 4:14, *KJV*). With encouragement from my mom, I, like Esther, have come to realize I have been personally called to reach the people around me.

> From observing my mother in church, I learned the importance of women leaders.

Being the middle child, I was often told by elders I had some sort of syndrome—middle child syndrome. My mother said I was born envious of my sister because she will always be the first and oldest. My mom also claimed I grew to resent my younger brother because he took my place as the baby. I have not ascribed to either perception, yet I have learned some invaluable lessons as the middle child.

The birth order did not bother me as much as the responsibility that came along with it. I thought the oldest one in the family held the role of leader of all things, but not in my family. My older sister is a kind, gentle spirit and collaborator. My younger brother is the free-spirited and adventurous child. I, on the other hand, am the independent thinker and natural-born leader in the family.

My siblings always looked to me as the decision maker in the family. I was the one who decided everything from where we would go to dinner for family outings to whose house we would gather for holidays and everything in between. My parents also looked to me to be the responsible one for all types of decisions from financial planning, estate planning and health, medical and retirement decisions.

A few years ago, my parents went on their first international cruise. I took them to meet the cruise ship and before my mother got out of the car she handed me a shoebox with instructions to open it should anything happen to them while away. I later learned upon their return that the box contained some cash and important paperwork concerning their final requests. Had I known what was in the box before they departed I may not have easily accepted it.

She always cautioned me to accept leadership as a privilege and not as a burden.

I remember questioning my role countless times through the years. I pouted and had childlike tantrums every time I was asked to take a leadership role. Eventually, I took my heed to my mom's advice. She always cautioned me to accept leadership as a privilege and not as a burden. The privilege of leadership is now one I willfully accept and honor. I now realize leadership is indeed a blessing I treasure. My leadership role in my family contributed to my leadership success professionally as well. I have a career that enables me to build relationships, engage communities and impact lives.

The Power of Living Life by Design

As a teenager, my sister and I grew up doing everything together until it came to dating. My parents allowed us to go out in groups at the age of 15 and eventually alone with a guy at the age of 16. Like most parents, mine had their own set of arbitrary rules.

When it became my time to entertain company, I recall getting into an argument with my dad one weekend over a guy. I cannot even remember what we debated about but I do remember telling my dad, "I'll never marry a preacher." Somehow I thought my children could have a better childhood than mine if their father was not a man of the cloth. While the words just rolled off my tongue at the time, it is the first time I can recount how badly words can sting. With tears in his eyes, my dad replied, "Was it that bad? Was it really that bad?" My words hurt him more than I could have ever imagined.

Wow! Looking back on things my childhood was wonderful, in my opinion, and not as bad as I thought it was at the time. My siblings and I did not have the crazy rules others assumed we had in a ministry-minded household. For some reason, people outside the church assumed we had an ultra-conservative and strict childhood but we were no different than any other family. In some houses of worship, women were shunned and forced to follow a lot of rules for apparel and decorum. This was not the case in our household. My sister and I were allowed to wear pants and we could wear makeup too. We did and still do listen to secular music and we even went to see PG- and R-rated movies. Of course, profanity was not allowed and we were taught to respect everyone we encountered. Our childhood was pretty normal now that I know better.

My childhood was also very special. Watching my parents interact had an incredible impact on my life. They are perfect examples of staying the course and going the distance. My relationship with my dad set the standard for what I want in a mate—how he should treat me and what I should expect in return. When I started dating in my teens, I was somewhat naive to think every man I met would treat me as my dad did. I was so wrong. I learned people are only products of their environments.

No matter how many times I get hurt, I still believe in love.

Some men I dated simply did not know how to treat me. Others were too insecure or arrogant. For others, we were just not compatible for various reasons. In any case, I am still a hopeless romantic. No matter how many times I get hurt, I still believe in love. I believe love feels good. I believe love can last forever. I believe a prince will someday come along with the royal qualities and characteristics of my dad, befitting of making me a queen.

My mom always took her role as a queen seriously. She definitely ruled the nest as we grew up. In 2012, while others were happily preparing for the holiday season, my family had just received devastating news. Just two weeks after surviving what could have been a tragic car accident and only two days before Thanksgiving, our beloved queen had been diagnosed with stage 1 breast cancer. Unlike two years prior when her mammogram results came back abnormal, her follow-up appointment was not cancelled by her doctor this time.

The week following Thanksgiving, we learned the prognosis was good—one surgery followed by radiation and that season would soon be over. Two months later, surgery came and went and so did the original treatment plan. Following surgery, more cancerous cells were found and she would need chemotherapy followed by a second surgery before having radiation. Our excitement over a speedy process was short-lived. A two-month plan quickly turned into eleven long months of more questions and unknown answers as we witnessed loss of hair and energy coupled with loss of tears.

And thus the real journey of resilience began for my family. The first family who once prayed for others was now standing in the need of prayer. The first lady who often asked God to use her did not expect God would choose to use her quite like that. We had lived our entire lives ministering to others and suddenly found ourselves in need of prayer—just like everyone else. Our faith was tried and tested. In the end, my mom survived cancer, my family survived the test and we learned what it meant to be resilient first hand.

In the midst of that crisis, I found myself ministering to my mother with the same words of wisdom she gave me years prior. After suddenly losing a job one day without warning, my mother calmly advised me, "We don't do all this talk about faith not to have any." She went on to encourage me to pray and seek guidance from God believing things would work out for my good. After surviving six months of unemployment on two months of savings, I not only gained the new role I desired but I found increased strength, perseverance and determination. Through my mother's illness and my own trials, I found out what it really meant to have joy in the midst of sorrow.

Pursue Resilience

- **Share Your Story.** As a closet introvert, I am a very private person. There are still some things my best friend does not know about me. While I have many acquaintances, there are few people in my life who really know my heart and soul. I tend to keep everything to myself, rarely lamenting to others about my problems and concerns, although I have many. I typically never cry either...that was until I started writing.

  With every written word, I share a tear from my heart. Every prose is an expression of emotion. By sharing with one another, we reveal our hidden vulnerabilities, express our mutual admiration of each other and free ourselves of the things that bind us. At Spelman, Dr. Johnetta B. Cole specifically taught us a principle of leadership that continues to guide me today: "The ultimate expression of generosity is not in giving of what you have but in giving of who you are."[1] Share your story and share it often. You never know how your story can help someone else along their journey of resilience.

- **Forgive.** Forgiveness, unlike an apology, is not for the offender but for you. It releases you from the pain of the one who hurt you whether you receive an apology or not. When we fail, and we will often, the first person we need to forgive is ourselves. If others have offended us, we must forgive them equally. Despite the many things we could do to punish or retaliate, none of them will satisfy hurt or take away the pain of the past. My responsibility, whenever treated unfairly, regardless of the circumstances, is to forgive. Forgiveness is an action of the heart. It only involves letting go of the anger, hurt and resentment in your spirit. Forgiveness will manifest itself in the way you talk and interact with others.

- **Faith, Family and Friendship Matter**. Through every situation I have encountered in life, there are three things that have sustained me—faith, family and friendships. The first gift my parents gave me as child was a foundation of faith. Matthew 17:20 (ref., *KJV*) tells us, "If you have faith the grain of a mustard seed, nothing will be impossible for you."[4] My belief in God, His humanity and His sovereignty give me hope for the future.

  The support of my family and friends is valued priceless to me. They are always present as cheerleaders, encouraging me daily and always believing in me. Sometimes we agree and at others times, quite frankly, they annoy me. Regardless of the circumstance or situation, I still love my family, and friends do matter to me.

Living Life by Design

- **Trust Your Gut.** It has often been said the intuition of a woman is powerful. As women, we have the rare and innate ability to sense when something is wrong, something "ain't right" or when something smells fishy. Often called discernment by church folk and emotional intelligence by psychologists, the intuition of a woman predicts the presence of danger and protects us from lurking predators.

  Through trial and error, I have learned to follow the advice of my grandmother, "Go with your first mind, baby." I have also adopted the wisdom of Maya Angelou, "When people show you who they are, believe them, the first time."[2] I have learned to trust my gut, that little voice that whispers in my ear telling me to STOP, DROP and ROLL. Stop my engagement. Drop my present company. Roll on to a new environment. Trust your gut.

- **Less Is More.** I used to think more was better. I wanted more clothes, more shoes, more friends, more fun and just more stuff. I accumulated lots of stuff, business cards, associates and calendar invites. I eventually ran out of time and space to accommodate the stuff and the people.

  Over time and through experience, I have learned quality counts above quantity. It is not about the number of things I possess or the number of people I know. My relationships are now based on worth and value. Not everyone who asks for my time deserves it. Just because items look and feel nice does not mean I should bring them home.

  When you take the time to purge the unnecessary people and things in your life, you will have more time and space to focus on what really matters the most. You will have less drama, stress and clutter, thereby making room for more love, peace and blessings. One day you will look back and wonder why you ever thought you needed all the stuff and people anyway. One day you will realize that less really is more.

Works Cited

[1] **Wikipedia. (2015).** Johnnetta B. Cole. In "Volunteer Opportunities." www.sandiego.gov; accessed October 5, 2011. Retrieved August 23, 2015 from https://en.m.wikipedia.org/wiki/Johnnetta_B._Cole

[2] **Oprah Winfrey Network. (2013).** http://www.huffingtonpost.com/2013/03/14/oprah-life-lesson-maya-angelou_n_2869235.html

With over 15 years of experience in philanthropic and nonprofit positions in the Greater Philadelphia area, and a lifetime of leadership and paying it forward, **Mellanie Kai Lassiter** is a renaissance relationship manager skilled in linking people in need with people who care. Her success in building relationships, program development, and working and communicating effectively with media, corporate and civic leaders has positioned her as a leader in corporate social responsibility. Driven by purpose and not position, her propensity for personally investing in individuals has made her a true champion of people.

Mellanie is someone who looks to empower individuals and communities by planting seeds for advancement, as evidenced by the weekly updates to her blog that touch on topics from how to be an effective leader to forgiveness and the dynamics of interpersonal relationships. *"My Best Selfie Yet"* is the theme of her writing. With it, Mellanie seeks to 'empower and uplift' people by encouraging them to live their best life and be the best version of themselves, based on Christian principles.

Mellanie is the daughter of a second generation pastor, an aunt to a niece and nephew, and a friend and mentor to many. She is a proud member of Alpha Kappa Alpha Sorority, Inc., and the Philadelphia Chapter of The Links, Inc. She holds an undergraduate degree from Spelman College and a Master of Training and Organization Development from St. Joseph's University.

To follow her weekly musings, visit MellanieLassiter.com.

ELEVEN

REACHING BEYOND YOUR LIMITATION TO YOUR GOD-GIVEN POSSIBILITIES

BY TERESITA GLASGOW

Defining Resilience

Leaders love lemonade, because as the saying goes, "When life gives you lemons, make lemonade." There are no lessons learned in life that are not valuable in some way. Even our mistakes help us grow in ways we never could have imagined. I am a lifelong learner because I realize things are constantly changing. There is nothing too trivial or too difficult that I will not seek to learn from. Life is full of challenge and opportunity—sometimes they are opposite sides of the same coin and it is only one's perspective that determines the outcome—but it takes resilience to stay the course. Resilience is that burst of energy that pushes you forward in spite of the desire to quit.

My Story

When I was a child I felt at times as though I had been robbed, that something was missing. I did not understand why I lived with my grandparents instead of my mother. As an adult, I realize that without my grandparents' intervention, without their love and care, I would be a completely different person. But because of my wrong thinking and immaturity, after high school I moved out of my grandparents' home in Washington, D.C. and moved with my mother who lived in Harlem, New York. I quickly began to ignore all of the lessons and training my grandparents taught me—after all, I was grown, and besides, they were old-fashioned and times had changed.

Life seems to have a way of course correcting and eventually the lessons I learned from my grandparents and the lack of comfortable living overshadowed my reasons for leaving home. By that time I was a single parent of two and life was difficult, but because I had not grown up in that environment I knew life could be better. I remembered who I was based on what my grandparents told me. I remembered their encouragement. Life had dragged me down but it could not count me out. I began to allow new, positive information in and to accept that my grandparents had been right all along.

Life seems to have a way of course correcting...

What I know now that I did not know back then is there are basic, fundamental truths in life that govern everything and when decisions go against those truths, difficulties usually follow.

For instance, an airplane can fly, but if an individual leaps off the top of a building the law of gravity will immediately kick in and she will swiftly fall to her death. Why is the plane able to fly? Doesn't gravity also cause it to fall? The law of gravity applies to both, however there are other laws that supersede gravity, which is what allows the plane to fly. Our limiting beliefs, like gravity, pull us down and prevent us from reaching our full potential. However, when we introduce the right beliefs, which surpass those limiting beliefs, we are able to fly to higher heights.

In my situation my limiting beliefs in my youth were due to my immaturity and an overactive imagination. I did not know my life was caught up in the consequences of someone else's poor decisions. My mind could not fathom all the different reasons why I lived with my grandparents, why my father was not in my life or why my mother lived so far away, and I allowed my imagination to create stories, or scripts, to fill in the blind spots. These blind spots were my limiting beliefs that framed my own poor decisions, becoming a hindrance to my resilience.

Our limiting beliefs, like gravity, pull us down and prevent us from reaching our full potential.

In life we all write our own personal scripts or stories based on the information we have. Unfortunately, not all that information is true or complete. When we make decisions based on incorrect or limited information, the outcomes are usually faulty. As a result, the characters in our scripts are all mixed-up — sometimes the people we choose to ignore are the ones we should be listening to and the ones we choose to follow are the ones we should not follow at all.

Throughout our life journey we learn from mentors or from mistakes. During that period of my life I learned by making many mistakes because of following the wrong mentors. That was a long time ago and more than ever I am grateful for my grandparents' training. It was their teachings that emerged after I lived life on my own terms and made a mess of it.

Recognizing and Removing the Enemies of Resilience

When I listen to people like Anthony Robbins, Willie Jolley or Les Brown tell of their challenges and difficulties I am amazed. They remind me that inside each of us is a power to overcome if we are willing to tap into it. Many times when we see successful people we think of them as they are now, but it is the difficult experiences they have overcome that make them who they are today.

Many times when we see successful people we think of them as they are now, but it is the difficult experiences they have overcome that make them who they are today.

I began to realize that many of my life scripts were lies and I had traded a secure middle-class environment for a life of poverty and despair. It was a period of one bad decision after another, but even the things I learned during those years of rebellion proved to be invaluable. In some respects those experiences helped me mature in ways I never would have otherwise, and they gave me the toughness I needed to change. Along with limiting beliefs, faulty thinking proved to be another enemy of resilience.

The thing about limiting beliefs is that when they are confronted by truth, many times they disappear, but they can leave residue. The residue may show up as thoughts later in life, as the pattern takes a while to correct.

Self-awareness, self-confidence and a willingness to learn replaced my inexperience and naiveté, and ultimately, my faulty thinking and limiting beliefs. My willingness to learn became a desire to attend college and a lifelong pursuit of learning. Although I was an adult with two small children by then, I knew the life we were living at that time was not the life I wanted for us. The principles and wisdom I learned as a child from my grandparents—the ones I ignored before—were still there below the surface. I reconnected to my childhood faith and began to grow spiritually.

Turning Reactions into Resilience

The scripts we write in our own minds are based on information and exposure, and that eventually brings change. Once I had the right information and the willingness to learn, my life changed dramatically. I quit my job as a hairdresser, attended and graduated from college and entered the world of financial services. During that time I received welfare and worked part-time. I guess living in New York and being a hairdresser in the Wall Street area made financial services a likely choice for me. My new script was the American Dream.

Life offers many lessons to be learned and taught. Ironically, when I worked in corporate America some of the rules I learned in Harlem applied better than a formal education.

Ironically, when I worked in corporate America some of the rules I learned in Harlem applied better than a formal education.

I began a career in corporate trust, a highly specialized area of financial services. It became more than just a job for me; it was my way up and my way out. I thrived in the environment. Each year I learned more, and each year I was rewarded. My colleagues began calling me Ms. Corporate Trust because I always studied the industry and was eager to share what I knew with others. Everything, including my life as a single parent, changed for the better because of my success in my career. I was set; my part in the American Dream was realized. In 1999, I was given an opportunity of a lifetime, or so I thought. I was working diligently on a project the office had all come to know as "Project Breakthrough." My colleagues and I felt a better name would have been "Project Breakup" because it would change our lives. For the first time in its existence our business was changing to accommodate the growing need for a way to do business at lower cost.

While several areas of the business had changed, including amended or revised laws, for the most part how things were done within the banks or trust companies remained the same. But the advent of technology, mergers and acquisitions caused a huge shift and trustees were scrambling to try to stay in the game. The fees trustees earned were at an all-time low while expenses were at an all-time high. With every advance of technology the trustee's income decreased. Project Breakthrough was supposed to be the answer for the problems impacting the industry.

The idea was innovative but I did not like it. I started my career as a securities clerk and had learned everything about the industry. I took pride in working on the bond deals from their beginning to their maturity. I enjoyed working with the issuers, the attorneys, the rating agencies and the others involved. The new procedures outlined in Project Breakthrough did not fit into the way I wanted corporate trust to be. Everything was cut up into chunks so that no one really needed to be a specialist and I was already a certified corporate trust specialist (CCTS). Instead of taking a bond deal from soup to nuts, so to speak, a different person was responsible for each aspect of the bond deal. It was more like an assembly line.

Later that year, when my bank asked me if I would consider moving to Atlanta, Ga., to help with a new book of business they had acquired, I said yes. For me it was an answer to prayer. While New York would soon implement Project Breakthrough, it would not happen in Georgia for the next two years. Though I knew Project Breakthrough was the wave of the future, it took away everything that made the industry interesting.

I moved to Georgia full of optimism. I visited the new office prior to moving and everyone seemed great. I anticipated fitting right in, but after my move I was confronted with hostility. I tried to make the situation work but after a while it was obvious they were upset about the acquisition and there was no way they were ever going to accept me.

They were hurt, and felt betrayed by their trust company that had sold its book of corporate trust business to the larger out-of-town bank. On top of that, they sent this stranger, whom they did not need, to work with them. They saw me as a spy. What is funny is that at the time I did not see it. I kept trying to be friendly and warm while doing my job. It did not work, so when another bank in Atlanta wanted to interview me I accepted the opportunity.

I got the job, said my goodbyes and moved into my new position. I bought a house and thought I could finally relax and just work on my job in an industry I absolutely loved. By then I had been in the industry for fifteen years and life was good. I was a vice president, a CCTS and a relationship manager.

Looking back over my life, I could not help but thank God for His goodness and faithfulness. I always viewed my move to Atlanta as a blessing from God. I did not understand what happened with the other position, but I felt that my moving on was for the best.

> Looking back over my life, I could not help but thank God for His goodness and faithfulness.

My first day on the new job was exciting, and my new boss seemed great. I did not notice the tension in the office; I was too busy trying to get acclimated to an entirely new bank. They had a different way of doing things but I was an expert at industry standards so I was not concerned. I had worked on many mergers and acquisitions of different bank trust companies so I knew I could do the work. I never had a problem fitting in anywhere except the last position that had very different circumstances.

My boss interviewed and hired my assistant. I thought that was a little strange, as I would have liked to conduct the interview myself since I would be working closely with the individual. I decided it did not really matter. I later found my assistant to be incompetent —the assistant had lied to get the position—and I was given a replacement.

During my first week I realized there was another vice president who was on vacation. When she returned the following week, she was very nice but was surprised to see me. As we talked I found out she was being harassed by our boss and felt I had been hired to replace her. That was a surprise to me; I did not know she existed until I was hired. Unfortunately, she was right. It turned out the previous vice president had been harassed and resigned. Now my new boss was trying to replace the current vice president, who technically was still an employee, by hiring me and harassing her until she left. My boss' plan worked—the other vice president resigned.

I did not know it then but I was about to enter one of the most difficult times in my life. I had come a long way from where I started out on my career journey. My limiting beliefs did not include corporate trust because I knew my craft, but I was not used to or experienced in all of the drama and sabotage. Years before, one of my mentors told me to "stay clear of the politics" and I listened to him. I had no desire to be a part of anything other than a professional career. Although I tried as hard as I could to stay clear of the drama, I had landed in drama central.

Over the next two years my boss subjected me to some really crazy antics—it was ridiculous. For example, since all new business was filtered and assigned by my manager, she did everything possible to prevent me from getting new clients and new deals. I knew by the end of the fiscal year my numbers would be low because all I would have to show was repeat business from my existing clients.

When I first began my career I learned not to live up to other people's expectations...

When I first began my career I learned not to live up to other people's expectations, especially those who did not want me to achieve my God-given possibilities. I knew God had not brought me that far to take me back again, so when I received an email for the newly forming Capital Markets Diversity Counsel, I applied and was accepted. The email stressed the fact that no approval from a manager was required. It seemed the bank knew it had some diversity problems and needed the employees to have the freedom to join without any backlash. While I was kept from achieving and sabotaged in the office, on the diversity counsel I was allowed to excel. That was exactly what I needed to keep my sanity, but because I had been oppressed for so long, I initially wondered if I could do it.

Serving as a member of the Capital Markets Diversity Counsel gave me the opportunity to have visibility throughout the bank and also looked good for my office. Not only was I an active part of the counsel, I was the only black, female vice president. There was only one problem—my boss had no control over it. The harassment at work increased and intensified.

During the next year, serving on the diversity counsel was a highlight of my career. We were able to complete several projects. For one day a month I was able to contribute something good for the employees and the bank. That one day felt wonderful, but the rest of the month my time at work was hell. The diversity counsel met in Charlotte, N.C., and my boss demanded I drive from Atlanta, Ga., to Charlotte, N.C. Fortunately, the counsel was made up of senior management and the senior vice president of capital markets insisted I fly using his cost center. Each positive contribution I made was met back in my office with heightened harassment.

It was not easy, but I managed to leave with my dignity intact.

Eventually my boss had her way and I was forced to resign. It was not easy, but I managed to leave with my dignity intact. After seventeen years in the industry, it was over. I had a good career that ended too early because there are evil people in the world. I decided to just move on, and instead of returning to New York, I opted to stay in Atlanta. Remaining in Atlanta meant leaving the profession that had given me the American Dream.

Transitions are tough because you are not exactly where you want to be, but you are not where you once were. As I moved into the next phase of my life I had to deal with negative emotions and rejection, although I knew my experience was not one hundred percent about me. I knew a lot of the challenges I confronted on my last job were due to the personal struggles my boss faced and the unwillingness of the bank to deal with them honestly. Either way, my challenge became confronting the current situation that was moving me into uncharted territory. It required an entire life makeover. Another part of the challenge was my age. I was no longer that adventurer who knew there was time—time to return to school, time to reach goals and enjoy the fruit of my labor. I was starting over at fifty.

After a while I understood I had been forced to face my destiny.

The challenge I had to deal with more than anything else was the ideas in my mind. I had to sort out and define what it was I loved so much about corporate trust. Thankfully, I had many transferable skills. Even though I set out on my quest to rebuild my life and redefine myself, not based on what I did but on who I was, I needed a stable income in order to do that. It took a while to find steady employment but it eventually came in the form of a contract job.

The year I resigned, I began a new business to inspire, inform and empower individuals to reach beyond their limitations to their God-given possibilities through Christian training and development. I also wrote and published my first book. My dream was to help others because I remembered my difficulties in the early days. I knew how hard it was to come up against limiting beliefs and what it took to overcome them. For me it seemed like a natural progression to help others overcome their obstacles. My contract job was perfect because it allowed me the time I needed to work on my dream. I was able to continue focusing on my company and to write and publish.

After a while I understood I had been forced to face my destiny. I knew my life would have been very different had I not followed my passion before and moved to Atlanta. Part of me longed for the stability of my old life, but part of me thrived in the adventure of my new life. Although I was over fifty and the transition had been involuntary, I recognized the divine orchestration and I am thankful.

The Power of Living Life by Design

At an earlier time in my life I made a decision to change and at a later time in my life I was forced to change. Both times required me to think differently, and both times required me to find strength in myself I did not know existed. When I think of my manager now, all I can say is, "Thank you." I realize what she saw in me frightened her because of her own insecurities. Each time I publish a book or speak, I know it was her false accusations that led to my supernatural promotion. The haters in your life should empower you because they see something in you that you may not see in yourself. If they are given the opportunity to harm you it will only work out for your good. Now I know to shout when I have a hater because something good is about to happen.

The haters in your life should empower you because they see something in you that you may not see in yourself.

Never return evil for evil. Remain respectful even when someone stands toe to toe with you and lies in your face. It is not easy to do but it has its rewards.

Stay focused on what you want out of life. When that gets blurry, which it sometimes will, especially in transitions, hold on to the last event, person, saying or experience you had that made you feel good. After a while you will regain your focus and drive to move forward.

Of all the valuable lessons that I have learned in life the most important is to say a prayer and keep it moving. *Never give up.*

Pursue Resilience

- Challenge every negative thought by seeking positive thoughts and information to meditate on.

- Seek to correct an erroneous self-image by creating the 'you' that you choose to be and not allowing others to define who you are.

- Grow through following your dreams by allowing each new relationship, skill or piece of information to expand and increase you.

Living Life by Design

- Focus on what you desire.
- Do not allow others to write your life script.
- Believe you can achieve your dream.

Teresita Glasgow is an author, inspirational speaker, radio talk show host, minister, mentor and savvy social media strategist. She is president and CEO of In His Season, Inc., a Christian Training and Development Company with an award winning monthly newsletter and a blog for contemporary Christian Thought, Salt & Light.

Her book, *Destiny: Seven Steps to Finding and Fulfilling Your Purpose in Life*, has influenced countless numbers to pursue their God-given destiny. It is her drive and tenacious "never give up" attitude along with her grounded and unshakable faith that took her from a life of despair as a single parent on welfare to a Wall street career as a Certified Corporate Trust Specialist.

Although her signature can be found on bond deals worth millions of dollars, it is her determination to see others accomplish their God given assignment that has become the driving force behind her writing, speaking and the leadership of In His Season, Inc.

Because of the wealth of her unique life experiences, Teresita is equipped to share a perspective that is practical and yet profound.

Connect with Teresita at TeresitaGlasgow.com.

TWELVE

BLESSING IN DISGUISE
BY VALERIA ROBINSON-BAKER

Defining Resilience

As true as time, everything must change; consequently, it is the only constant in life. Change and your reactions to its impact will be the one concept you must learn to embrace, therefore capitalizing on the opportunities it presents. The most significant opportunity it provides is your part in shaping the outcomes of your life. The ability to embrace transformation is a skill learned. How you adjust to the challenges of life are descriptive of being resilient. To define resilience includes perseverance, determination, optimism, commitment, empowerment and personal growth as a journey. These are just a few, but clearly definitive terms that explain what it takes to be resilient.

It is very much like the theory of evolution in regard to mammals that remains applicable today. Just as human physical growth occurs in a series of stages, which can be seen in the evolution from childhood to adulthood, change as it applies to an adult happens in a series of stages whereby the individual has a chance to sculpt the outcome. During the modification phase, you will become more enlightened through your development of new skills and facets of your personality that would have never been possible without the imposed adjustment. Revision creates resilience.

Within progression lies the blessings. Positive personal growth comes in several disguises eventually revealed through the challenges change presents. The disguises of clear core values, belief in oneself and mental toughness are the foundation to becoming resilient. These are facets of your personality that mirror character and strength. Along the way, time for reflection on lessons learned is essential. A necessity is time, time carved out on a frequent basis for self-reflection and self-inventory. At some point you are able to recognize your advancement, reflecting a toughness in moving through difficult situations repeatedly, coming out on the other side of the challenge stronger, smarter and more positive about the outcome.

The impact of change is personal, and I have learned that irrespective of how negative the circumstance, perception holds the greater mantle in the outcome. Difficulty is subjective. During my adversities, I held tightly to my intentions to eliminate the time wasted on self-pity. Instead, I attempted to receive the challenging situation with the anticipation of the lesson learned and keeping my determination intact. It was then that I was able to exact some control over my tragedies and disappointments. It was imperative I defined my future, not my circumstances. Choosing to have the upper hand in determining who I would be, I had to ask myself, "How do I move forward?" You too must ask who or what will determine your legacy and your footprint. Unexpected misfortunes occur in everyone's life. Will it be your circumstances or will it be you who defines your mark? Here is where your definition of resilience is derived. I have created my definition, now you create your own.

My Story

Learning to cope with pain and tragedy occurred early in life with the death of my father when I was eleven years old. It changed every aspect of my personality. Much of my capability to handle life's curve balls was learned through my parents and their perspectives on life. I was blessed to have their guidance. I watched how they handled life's misfortunes. Expectations of being strong and giving your best were established early on. I knew self-control was valued in our family and my actions had consequences. Each of us was counted upon to do our part in the absence of a father.

There were sayings my father would frequently repeat about difficult times such as "time heals all wounds"; "there is always a silver lining to every dark cloud"; and of course, "blessings in disguise." He made those sayings seem so resolute and absolute. I held those expressions close in my dark times. They brought me hope and comfort. Hope is what gets you through the challenges in life. I am sure you have a family member who passes along words of wisdom and love that you can repeat when you feel lost, alone or without direction. Use them. They are food for the soul and they will fill your heart when nothing else can.

> Hope is what gets you through the challenges in life.

My journey has taken me through many expected and unexpected twists and turns in life. No matter how much you plan, the unexpected will happen. You strive for educational degrees, jobs, promotions, marriage, children, a home, or success at home, church and work. Frequently when you are prepared for an opportunity, it seamlessly happens. At other times it does not happen regardless of your preparations or connectedness. It is just not meant to be. You will have to accept some things are not meant for you. However, you find there is a reason it did not occur. When a greater opportunity or better personality fit comes your way, your gut instincts tell you the situation is right, the healthy choice for you. Trust your gut instincts. They will never fail you!

Life has also taught me to be careful what I ask for; I just might get it. Translated, you often get more than you bargained for or more than you possibly could see on the other side of the dream. I married a physician (gastroenterologist) and we have two beautiful daughters. I served as a director of pharmacy, taught at pharmacy schools, was active in my community and yet I still felt a void in the frenzy called my life. I cherished my husband and his accomplishments, but life as the wife of a physician left many empty evenings alone as he built his business.

He started as a solo-practicing physician. Being solo meant he was on call every night after working a full day at the practice. He had no help in covering his practice 24 hours a day. At the time, it was a given in starting a practice alone. He was only home to rest, and that could and would be interrupted in the middle of the night if a patient were in need. I went to every hospital in town—there were six hospitals in the area at that time—attempting to be with him as much as I could while working and caring for our family. I understood that could happen, as I had witnessed his schedule while we dated during his residency and fellowship. It is different, however, when you are married expecting to have your partner there to share in the daily aspects of life. Yet that is the life of physicians, entrepreneurs, pro-ball players, or any professionals whose responsibilities exceed the limited expectations of a 9-5 job.

Despite my professional demands, I had to modify my perspectives and stand in the commitment to our plans for our family. The blessing is my children have strong values and are pending professionals because I was available while showing them a strong work ethic and providing structure to our family life. It was at a personal cost and was not easy, but it was worth every moment!

Recognizing and Removing the Enemies of Resilience

Each chapter in your life begins with an ending of a previous chapter. Interestingly enough, my youngest daughter had this meaningful and beautiful rite of passage as her class transitioned from middle school students to high school students. "Turning the Page" was the name of the proclaimed passage. It served as a remarkable living and maturity testimony of their first year in high school. It was a journey I found revealing and thought-provoking, as it allowed each child to self-reflect.

Reflection offers you time to measure where you are in relation to the vision you have for your life.

As adults, we too must slow down and make time for reflection. Find quiet time to determine what you have learned from your past experiences and how have you turned the page to each chapter in your life. In doing so, you can identify the enemies of resilience and ensure your strength is greater than the enemy because of the values and lessons learned along your journey. Reflection offers you time to measure where you are in relation to the vision you have for your life. Do you need to change direction? Are you asking and doing enough to move yourself closer to your goals?

The enemies of resilience are time wasters: lack of vision, lack of discernment with friends and associates, giving up, feeling as if a failure defines you, believing your circumstances define you, lack of control and ultimately a lack of perspective. Failure often is the biggest culprit in stealing most people's dreams of becoming their best selves. For the multitudes, one failure gets them stuck and many letdowns will have them stamp "failure" on their foreheads. Defeat is a teacher. She teaches you how to do things differently, and every setback is a refocused step toward your best future. Do not allow a few drawbacks to steal your glory. I never met one that did not teach me something!

Turning Reactions into Resilience

Just when I thought I had overcome the major obstacles of life, death visited again and again. My mother passed in 2007 after a lengthy illness, and unexpectedly my soul partner, my brother, passed in 2011. My brother's death struck me extremely hard, as he was my confidant, my best friend and my protector. Life once again rocked my world. Losing him was as if I had lost my father all over again. I constantly cried every evening on my drive home from work. I would work until very late in the evenings to avoid suffering so much pain. It was the one time I found it difficult to push myself forward. I kept telling myself it was time to move forward.

I kept telling myself it was time to move forward.

Logically, I could not push through the discomfort. I pulled out all the self-help tools I knew to find direction. Realizing I was in a deepening hole, I had to stop the spiral. I went to counseling and listened to positive thinkers such as Joel Osteen, Louise Hay, Iyanla Vanzant and Rev. T.D. Jakes. Everything I could think of was used to hold on. To deaden the agony of thinking and breathing without him, I utterly sought strong, mental antidotes for relief.

I hope you learn something powerful from the sorrow exacted from the loss of a loved one. It was difficult for me to visit our family home of 40-plus years in Tallahassee, Fla. I had lost each and every one in my immediate family unit and the house was still too real of a reminder. I visited there infrequently, paying the bills for upkeep and maintenance. The residence used to be filled with love and treasured memories. With everyone gone, it was a shell of the vibrant life that once existed there. Pain emanated from the bottom of my heart each time I visited. It was clear I was not facing sorrow rationally. I had to embrace the change.

My insight said I needed to find closure, but how? The normal infrequent sips of my wonderfully pale pink Grey Goose Cosmopolitan cocktails became more like a weekend confidant than simple sips of joy when I drank them in the past. I was hiding the hurt in the sips of the drink. It helped me not to feel. I knew this had to stop and stop soon. Drinking numbed and masked the experience for a moment, a day or a night, however, the issues remained once the drink left my lips. And then the time came. The anguish of my brother not being with me subsided. It diminished more each day, each month and eventually each year.

In my discovery I found there are occurrences in life that can still throw you outside your comfort zone.

It took me three years to move forward. I was both impatient and patient with myself. In my discovery I found there are occurrences in life that can still throw you outside your comfort zone. Unmistakably, I was a bit out of control. I felt impatient with my self-correcting methods. However, I learned that sometimes only time can heal a loss.

It became obvious to me I was allowing my past to control my future. Therefore, I had to let go of the past. Remodeling the house and removing so many reminders from my family's Tallahassee property helped me heal. Most importantly, it helped save my life. I kept the pictures and memorabilia items to pass along to my children. It was only then I began to be patient and forgiving of myself and was able to move on. With the past put in its necessary place, the future was now more welcoming. Now I am "walkin' my talk" again and it feels good!

The Power of Living Life by Design

There is power in knowing life is meant to have complexities and purpose. It is by these complexities that character is built and where strength and drive are derived. Thirty years ago I did not understand I was living life by design. I knew the desired outcome. I sought out the people, experiences and opportunities that would partner with my dream. Visualization was key. Visioning and modeling behaviors viewed as leadership is how I patterned my life. I asked for more responsibilities and that yielded greater opportunities. With my professional growth and responsibilities it was appropriate to reach back and help others. I mentored others and served my community in a way that my mentees are now seasoned professionals. I am proud of my actions, trials and triumphs.

I accepted when I became the wife of a physician it would not be easy, but it would be fulfilling, and it has been. I had plenty of mentors around me to teach the realities of being married to a physician as well as being a woman and a professional. I also appreciated at 32 and 37 years old, respectively, I had given birth to two of the loveliest human gifts in the world, my daughters. My role has been to protect, lead and love them. You see, my choices were made as carefully as possible. My desire was to have lived in a manner in which I served as captain of my ship. Of course, there were mistakes along the way. Blunders are to be used as lessons. For the most part, I have been the CEO of my lifespan and destiny. I recognize I lived life on purpose.

Now that my daughters are close to ending their college years, they remember their youth and my involvement. They recall their spring breaks where time was spent with family and friends in exotic and not-so-exotic places and the joy for that moment in time.

They also have memories of me juggling work to make their school activities. I had my share of challenges along the way—death, my health challenges, rearing teenage daughters, marriage and pressures of being a director of pharmacy. But that is the reality of today. I signed up for the game.

Do not think your trials are any greater or less than anyone else's. God is faithful. He will not let you be tempted beyond your abilities or what you can bear. Instead, with the temptation, God will also supply a way out so you will be able to endure it (ref. 1 Corinthians 10:13, *KJV*). Know you will get through it. The blessing is when you discover how to receive the tasks in your life as gifts of strength and grace. A blessing in disguise is always grace.

My dear sisters, your takeaways are:

Pursue Resilience

- Understand change is constant. Life happens. Use it to your benefit.
- Do not wallow in the unfortunate outcomes. Put your prettiest heels on and walk through the craziness in style and grace. If you cannot do the grace, please do the style!
- Persevere. Do not give up or in. Know your power is in rising up to meet your destiny.
- Define your legacy. Your circumstances are temporary and they do not define you.

Living Life by Design

- Live your life on purpose. Do not be afraid to fail. Failure just gives you more skills to come back and kick butt!
- Contemplate every choice you make; it affects the rest of your life. After all, it is a choice.
- Know what the life you want looks like and strive to achieve it.
- Use mentors to help you see the light. You are not in this alone. Do not be age selective! Look for supportive friends and family.

- Keep perspective of all that you have been blessed to have and be thankful. Count your blessings.
- Create your opportunities. You are the master of your ship. Create the pathways to your destination.
- Redesign as necessary; you are allowed self-corrections.
- Make yourself available to the next generation of movers and shakers.
- Do not be stingy with your knowledge.
- There are no mistakes unless you do not learn from them.
- Never stop learning.
- Know your value. Only you can determine your worth!
- Continue to reinvent yourself. Find new aspects of yourself and work them!

Valeria (Val) Robinson-Baker is a 1979 graduate of Florida A. & M. University College of Pharmacy and Pharmaceutical Sciences. She was formerly the Acting Quality Manager and presently the Sterile Production Supervising Pharmacist, overseeing the compliance with cGMP, USP <797> and <795> Standards of Performance for Olympia Compounding Pharmacy, an FDA Registered Outsourcing Facility.

Valeria has over two decades of expertise in pharmacy administration/management and hospital pharmacy practice. She received her Consultant Pharmacist license in 1984 and obtained certifications in Dyslipidemias, Vaccinations, Medication Therapy Management, Pharmacy Regulatory Specialist, with additional training in Women's Health Concerns and Bioidentical Hormone Replacement. Her expertise expands across a spectrum of Hospital Pharmacy Administration, Long-Term Care and Compounding Pharmacy practice.

A recipient of numerous awards, Valeria plays an active role in her community through many volunteer activities spanning her career. Her most recent community commitments are serving as President of the Orlando, FL. Chapter of The Links, Inc. (2015-2017), her 1999 appointed role on the Governor's Advisory Board on Diabetes for a three-year term under Governor Jeb Bush as well as serving on the boards of Hebni Nutrition Consultants, Inc. (1999-2009) and the Girls and Boys Clubs of Central Florida (2005-2010).

Valeria is married to Dr. Robert T. Baker, a practicing Gastroenterologist and Internist in the Central Florida area and they have two daughters, Brittney Alexa and Camille Victoria.

Contact her at vbaker4379@gmail.com

Closing Remarks and Exercises

Now Is Your Time to Step into the Amazing Life God Designed for You

Reading about resilience does not make one resilient. It comes about a lot like working out. What matters most is what you do day by day over time. And being resilient does not mean life's major hardships are not difficult or distressing. In my message at the beginning of this book, resilience is quoted as *an interactive product of beliefs, attitudes, approaches, behaviors and perhaps physiology that help people fare better during adversity and recover more quickly following it.* The key is to build on strengths, cultivate possibility and accept positive change—noticing how well you know yourself and endeavoring to successfully manage your thoughts. A thought may seem harmless, but if it becomes toxic, even just a thought can become physically, emotionally or spiritually dangerous.[1] This requires some work. Use the steps in these exercises to get you started on the change you seek.

Step 1. Discover what is in you.

People may identify themselves by their careers, positions, accomplishments or roles in society. Still some covet the personalities and activities of others. Living a lie is a surefire way to eventually become hurt and intensify adversity. You can have more character development, wealth creation, motivation and resilience when you discover what works well in you. Stop right now and dig deeply into your soul. Locate a quiet place and some quality time alone and listen to your heart for the divine whisper of who you are and the power you carry. What are you hearing? Write down the responses to the following:

a. Who am I? ________________________________

b. What brings me authentic joy? ____________________

c. What brings me inner peace? ____________________

d. Am I forgiving towards others? ____________________

Step 2. Sort your laundry.

Sometimes we allow unhelpful feelings and emotions to rule when in fact we actually have full control over them. Question what you believe about this. Assess anything causing you discomfort and distress. Be honest. This exercise is not going to remove the feeling but will bring you the understanding of how to get through it. Expressing your true emotions is a major step toward preparing the right mindset so you can outsmart your setback. Write them down here:

a. Its unhelpful and distressing when I feel ______________

   ____

   (*Example: unappreciated and unloved*)

b. This is unhelpful because ________________________

   ____

   (*Example: It causes me to engage in negative behaviors like "shopping therapy" or negative self-talk*)

c. The underlying belief I need to question is ________________

____

(*Example: Beauty is mostly about what size dress I am in*)

d. A more resilient response that can help me outsmart this is

____

(*Example*: *It is true I need to lose weight, but focusing on* exercising *and things I enjoy will keep me at my best*)

e. What are normally your first thoughts when you face a difficult situation? Are they toxic or healthy? Words follow thoughts. Actions follow thoughts.

____

____

(*Example: Reacting to an issue in the 'heat of the moment' can be toxic. Purposely deciding how to think and speak in a situation and choosing to speak only what you want is healthy.*)

f. I blame myself when: ___________________________________

____

g. I blame others when: ___________________________________

____

h. I always ask for help because: ___________________________

____

i. I never ask for help because: ____________________________

____

Step 3. Disarm unhelpful invaders.

Power comes to what you give it. You may feel angry about what has happened and even fearful about your future. Your aim is to focus on the desires of your heart and neutralize the victim mindset. Consider the answers to these questions:

a. What have I settled for? ______________________________

____

b. What excuses are blocking my path? ________________

____

c. Who must I forgive now? _______________________

Step 4. Give yourself a check-up.

Resilience comes with more ease when you are physically and psychologically healthy. Your welfare carries over into every area of your life. What are your beliefs, behaviors and attitudes concerning optimizing your physical, emotional and spiritual wellbeing?

Physical

a. Write here the date of your last physical exam with your doctor. ______________________ If you have not seen a doctor for the past two years, write here the reason why. ______________________________

b. Write here any physical concerns needing correcting now.

____

c. Write here your plan for handling your physical concerns.

d. Write here the date the steps were completed and how you feel now about this accomplishment.

e. Complete this sentence: I do not have difficulty eating healthy and exercising regularly because

Emotional

a. What are the top 3 things that easily irritate you and why?

b. I believe I have influence over these because I am/can/will

____

____

____

Spiritual

a. I am grateful for

____

____

b. Journal your gratitude list every day starting now.

c. I believe my faith deserted me during hard times because

____

____

____

Step 5. Define what matters most.

We learn more about ourselves when we answer thought-provoking questions like these:

a. What do I want? __________________________

____

b. What is important to me? ____________________

c. Who is important to me? ____________________

d. What drives you and gives you satisfaction? ______________

____

e. What do you value? ___________________________________

f. What would you sacrifice in order to have the life you want?

____

____

Review all of your responses and from them answer the following questions from my beginning message:

1. What is the hidden opportunity and where can it lead?
2. What has the setback shown you that needs changing?
3. What are the best lessons learned? How will you implement these lessons for change?
4. What will be your new normal?

Resilience must be intentional. To discover your values in action inventory of strengths, follow this link to access a courtesy survey: http://DrDeanaUnlimited.pro.viasurvey.org

Works Cited

[1]**Leaf, Dr. Carolyn**. 2009. "Who Switched Off My Brain: Controlling Toxic Thoughts and Emotions." Improv, Ltd., Southlake, Texas, pg. 13.

Dr. Deana Murphy is an international renowned award winning author, speaker and advocate for positive change who focuses on strategic implementation approaches to guide busy leaders in releasing their greatest potential in both their personal and professional lives. She is considered an expert in her field of 'lifestyle branding' and supports that everyone can cultivate possibility and be more efficient, effective and creative when they are happy and enjoy their lives. Under her brand, Dr. Deana Unlimited, she is a trusted advisor to entrepreneurs, corporate and medical professionals who seek ways to build on their strengths and create positive dynamics for the economy. She is a former adjunct university instructor, she writes for the Women and Third Metric divisions of *The Huffington Post, and* is recognized as one of the top minority business advocates in her region by *The Philadelphia Business Journal*. In 2012, *Exceptional People Magazine* included her in their list of top twenty exceptional business icons. Her research and advice has received attention from *CBN, O* (*Oprah*) *Magazine, Fine Living, HGTV, Panache Publication, Meredith Books, Empowering Everyday Women* and a variety of magazines, radio programs and podcast. She makes her home in eastern Pennsylvania.

46506944R00121

Made in the USA
Lexington, KY
06 November 2015